SEASONS OF FAITH

Adult Resource Book

Background for the Sunday Lectionary

Cycle B

Irene Nowell, OSB

Anne Marie Sweet, OSB

Jeanita F. Strathman Lapa
General Editor
Eleanor Suther, OSB

BROWN-ROA
A Division of Harcourt Brace & Company

Dubuque, Iowa

Nihil Obstat
    Rev. Richard L. Schaefer

Imprimatur
    ✠Most Rev. Daniel W. Kucera, O.S.B.
    Archbishop of Dubuque
    January 16, 1990

The Imprimatur is an official declaration that a book or pamphlet is free
of doctrinal or moral error. No implication is contained therein that
anyone who granted the Imprimatur agrees with the contents, opinions,
or statements expressed.

Acknowledgments

The development of this series was partially funded by:

   The Catholic Church Extension Society, Chicago, IL

   The Catholic Communications Campaign, New York, NY

   Mount Saint Scholastica Convent, Atchison, KS

   Archbishop's Fund for Sisters, Los Angeles, CA

   St. Joseph Foundation, Concordia, KS

   Social Justice Fund, Conventual Franciscan Friars, Midwest Province

and by smaller donations from over thirty bishops, dioceses, and religious communities who serve in small
town and country parishes.

Book Team

Publisher—Ernest T. Nedder
Editorial Director—Sandra Hirstein
Production Editor—Marilyn Bowers Gorun
Production Manager—Marilyn Rothenberger
Interior Design—Debra L. O'Brien, Cathy A. Frantz
Cover Design—Cathy A. Frantz
Cover Illustrations—Stanley J. Lapa, Jr., Judith McCully
Sunday Thematic Illustrations—Stanley J. Lapa, Jr., Judith McCully,
Jane Stembridge, Cathy A. Frantz
Journal Page Borders-Susan T. Staron

Photo Credits: James L. Shaffer—46, 106

ISBN 0–697–02894–1

10 9 8 7 6 5 4 3

IN THE BEGINNING

by: Dolores Curran

(from her book "In the Beginning There Were the Parents" published by Winston Press)

In the beginning there were the parents. They listened to the word and brought it home, where it shone forth at table, in the fields, and before the hearth. They spread the Good News from generation to generation as easily as they planted and harvested the seed.

They were a simple people, these ancestors of ours who tilled the land in Germany, tended the vineyards in Italy, and gathered potatoes in Ireland. They never studied a catechism, built a school, or heard of CCD. Yet they had a deep abiding Catholic faith. How could that be?

They lived their faith daily. They told time by the convent bells and bowed their heads in prayer at Angelus, wherever they were. Their whole village fasted in Lent and feasted on holy days. They married each other. For most, their whole world lay within their village, and that world went unchanged for centuries. Life was harsh, but faith was easy to pass on.

Then they crossed the ocean to the land of opportunity, America, and they were bewildered. New and alien forces attacked the family structure. The children began asking why they were different, and, faced with the fear of losing their children to this strange new culture, the parents turned to their Church.

They sought and received leadership from the pastor, the parish father. He advised them on many matters, from voter registration to preserving the faith of their children. Out of this leadership the Catholic schools were born.

In the middle there were the Theys—nuns, priest, schools. The parents relaxed. Parents concentrated on furnishing a better life for their families and left the job of religion to the Theys. They would teach the commandments. They would teach the children their prayers. They would baptize the children, run the schools, and preserve the faith of generations. And They did a magnificent job.

So the parents began doing less. No longer did they pray together as a family or sing together the old German hymns. When the school began to send the children to First Communion as a class, the family stopped celebrating it as a family milestone. When the school began teaching units on the saints, the family stopped having special name day festivities. Hundreds of ethnic customs were lost. Religious storytelling in the home became obsolete.

Eventually the parents forgot how to pass on the Word to their children. They forgot how to pray together as a family. They became embarrassed to sing together. They could no longer talk about God or religion comfortably.

So the blamed the Theys. Why weren't They teaching their children to pray, to believe, to accept, just as They had always done before? And the Theys— the priests, nuns, and directors of religious education — explained that They were no longer able to do it alone. Teaching religion in the classroom wasn't enough. To be lived, religion had to return to the family.

In the end there is the beginning, the Christian family. We are the parents, the beginning and the end of this saga. How we let Christ's words shine forth again at the table and in front of the TV set in our Future Shock culture will largely determine our children's present and future faith.

That is what this article is all about—the return to our rightful place as the first and foremost religious educators. Re-educating ourselves to become primary educators is a challenge, especially at this time in history. Life is easier, but faith is harder to pass on. Nevertheless, faith is still worth passing on, and our children still deserve to receive it. So let's make the commitment to them and begin.

Contents

Introduction v

Sundays throughout the Year	1990	1993	1996	1999	Page
First Sunday of Advent	Dec 2	Nov 28	Dec 1	Nov 28	1
Second Sunday of Advent	Dec 9	Dec 5	Dec 8	Dec 5	3
Third Sunday of Advent	Dec 16	Dec 12	Dec 15	Dec 12	5
Fourth Sunday of Advent	Dec 23	Dec 19	Dec 22	Dec 19	7
Feast of the Holy Family	Dec 30	Dec 26	Dec 29	Dec 26	9
	1991	**1994**	**1997**	**2000**	
Solemnity of the Epiphany	Jan 6	Jan 2	Jan 5	Jan 2	11
Feast of the Baptism of the Lord	Jan 13	Jan 9	Jan 12	Jan 9	13
Second Sunday in Ordinary Time	Jan 20	Jan 16	Jan 19	Jan 16	15
Third Sunday in Ordinary Time	Jan 27	Jan 23	Jan 26	Jan 23	17
Fourth Sunday in Ordinary Time	Feb 3	Jan 30		Jan 30	19
Feast of the Presentation	(Feb 2)	(Feb 2)	Feb 2	(Feb 2)	21
Fifth Sunday in Ordinary Time	Feb 10	Feb 6	Feb 9	Feb 6	23
Sixth Sunday in Ordinary Time		Feb 13		Feb 13	25
Seventh Sunday in Ordinary Time				Feb 20	27
Eighth Sunday in Ordinary Time				Feb 27	29
Ninth Sunday in Ordinary Time				Mar 5	31
First Sunday of Lent	Feb 17	Feb 20	Feb 16	Mar 12	33
Second Sunday of Lent	Feb 24	Feb 27	Feb 23	Mar 19	35
Third Sunday of Lent	Mar 3	Mar 6	Mar 2	Mar 26	37
Fourth Sunday of Lent	Mar 10	Mar 13	Mar 9	Apr 2	39
Fifth Sunday of Lent	Mar 17	Mar 20	Mar 16	Apr 9	41
Passion Sunday	Mar 24	Mar 27	Mar 23	Apr 16	43
Easter Sunday	Mar 31	Apr 3	Mar 30	Apr 23	49
Second Sunday of Easter	Apr 7	Apr 10	Apr 6	Apr 30	51
Third Sunday of Easter	Apr 14	Apr 17	Apr 13	May 7	53
Fourth Sunday of Easter	Apr 21	Apr 24	Apr 20	May 14	55
Fifth Sunday of Easter	Apr 28	May 1	Apr 27	May 21	57
Sixth Sunday of Easter	May 5	May 8	May 4	May 28	59
Ascension and Seventh Sunday of Easter	May 12	May 15	May 11	June 4	61

	1991	1994	1997	2000	
Solemnity of Pentecost	May 19	May 22	May 18	June 11	63
Trinity Sunday	May 26	May 29	May 25	June 18	65
Solemnity of Corpus Christi	June 2	June 5	June 1	June 25	67
Tenth Sunday of Ordinary Time	June 9		June 8		69
Eleventh Sunday in Ordinary Time	June 16	June 12	June 15		71
Twelfth Sunday in Ordinary Time	June 23	June 19	June 22		73
Thirteenth Sunday in Ordinary Time	June 30	June 26		July 2	75
Solemnity of Sts Peter and Paul	(June 29)	(June 29)	June 29	(June 29)	77
Fourteenth Sunday in Ordinary Time	July 7	July 3	July 6	July 9	79
Fifteenth Sunday in Ordinary Time	July 14	July 10	July 13	July 16	81
Sixteenth Sunday in Ordinary Time	July 21	July 17	July 20	July 23	83
Seventeenth Sunday in Ordinary Time	July 28	July 24	July 27	July 30	85
Eighteenth Sunday in Ordinary Time	Aug 4	July 31	Aug 3		87
Feast of the Transfiguration	(Aug 6)	(Aug 6)	(Aug 6)	Aug 6	89
Nineteenth Sunday in Ordinary Time	Aug 11	Aug 7	Aug 10	Aug 13	91
Twentieth Sunday in Ordinary Time	Aug 18	Aug 14	Aug 17	Aug 20	93
Twenty-First Sunday in Ordinary Time	Aug 25	Aug 21	Aug 24	Aug 27	95
Twenty-Second Sunday in Ordinary Time	Sept 1	Aug 28	Aug 31	Sept 3	97
Twenty-Third Sunday in Ordinary Time	Sept 8	Sept 4	Sept 7	Sept 10	99
Twenty-Fourth Sunday in Ordinary Time	Sept 15	Sept 11		Sept 17	101
Feast of the Triumph of the Cross	(Sept 14)	(Sept 14)	Sept 14	(Sept 14)	103
Twenty-Fifth Sunday in Ordinary Time	Sept 22	Sept 18	Sept 21	Sept 24	105
Twenty-Sixth Sunday in Ordinary Time	Sept 29	Sept 25	Sept 28	Oct 1	109
Twenty-Seventh Sunday in Ordinary Time	Oct 6	Oct 2	Oct 5	Oct 8	111
Twenty-Eighth Sunday in Ordinary Time	Oct 13	Oct 9	Oct 12	Oct 15	113
Twenty-Ninth Sunday in Ordinary Time	Oct 20	Oct 16	Oct 19	Oct 22	115
Thirtieth Sunday in Ordinary Time	Oct 27	Oct 23	Oct 26	Oct 29	117
All Saints and All Souls	(Nov 1/2)	(Nov 1/2)	Nov 1/2	(Nov 1/2)	119
Thirty-First Sunday in Ordinary Time	Nov 3	Oct 30		Nov 5	121
Thirty-Second Sunday in Ordinary Time	Nov 10	Nov 6		Nov 12	123
Dedication of St John Lateran	(Nov 9)	(Nov 9)	Nov 9	(Nov 9)	125
Thirty-Third Sunday in Ordinary Time	Nov 17	Nov 13	Nov 16	Nov 19	127
Solemnity of Christ the King	Nov 24	Nov 20	Nov 23	Nov 26	129

Introduction

The lectionary is the Church's formation program. As we read the selections from the Hebrew Scriptures or Old Testament and the New Testament and ponder their meaning as individuals and as a community, we enter more deeply into the mystery of Christ. Pondering Scripture over a lifetime, we gradually "put on the mind of Christ."

Sharing the word at Sunday worship has been the center of the Church's formation process from its very beginning. The process reaches back even further into our Jewish heritage. The Hebrew Scriptures or Old Testament tells stories of the renewal of the covenant in which the reading of the Law was an important element. The reading of the Scriptures in the assembly of believers formed the centerpiece of Jewish worship in the synagogue. A portion of the Scripture was read and reflected upon each week, apparently taking up where the reader from the previous week had left off.

In the beginning, early Christians continued to worship with the Jewish community at the synagogue. But in time they found themselves unwelcome in the synagogue and formed their own worshiping communities. They continued to follow the pattern of worship used in the synagogue, which included the reading of Scripture.

It was in such worshiping communities that the stories and sayings of Jesus were collected and retold. These communities also shared letters from their pastoral leaders. Certain letters, especially the letters of Paul, were read over and over, because the believers found in them an authentic expression of their experience of Christian faith. From such sharing, the books of the New Testament as we know them gradually took shape.

Since persons who could read were the exception rather than the rule, people listened to the Scriptures read in the assembly. As they listened to the word proclaimed, the word became a living Word, God's Word in their midst.

As time went on, the written word began to be seen as a canon, a measuring instrument for gauging the authenticity of one's faith. But the tradition was understood as broader than what had been written. The Bible itself was seen as the Church's book, which could not be interpreted apart from the community of believers which was its source.

Historians and archaeologists have discovered several ancient lectionaries which seem to have been used in early Christian communities. Christian communities of the first few centuries established their own systems of readings or lections. Some lectionaries were used throughout a particular region. With the massive reforms of the Council of Trent after the reformation, one lectionary was established for the whole Western Church. The lectionary used primarily New Testament readings rearranged to be repeated every year. This lectionary was in use until the revisions established by Vatican Council II.

Because they wanted to promote a better understanding of Scripture, the bishops of Vatican Council II called for a revision of the lectionary. The revision was to include more selections from the Bible, especially the Hebrew Scriptures or Old Testament. As a result, the current Roman lectionary was established, providing for a three-year cycle. In this new lectionary, the Gospels of Matthew, Mark, and Luke are read continuously, except for the seasons of Advent, Lent, and Easter. The first reading is chosen from the Hebrew Scriptures or Old Testament, the Acts of the Apostles, or the Book of Revelation. This reading is intended to harmonize with the gospel reading. The second readings each week are not necessarily related to either the Old Testament or the gospel reading, but form a continuous reading from the epistles.

The lectionary is the Church's curriculum, just as the liturgy is the Church's program of formation. Through the three-year cycle, the Church proposes for our reflection a broad range of readings which present the teachings of Jesus and the central mysteries of our faith. The homilist leads us to reflect upon our own experience to see what God is doing in our lives. As we listen to the story of what God has done for His people in the past, we can begin to tell our own stories of faith. Each time the Scriptures are read, we listen to them anew to see what God is saying to us at this time in our lives.

The Scriptures are ancient documents, written in another time for another situation. They record God's teaching of His people over fifteen hundred years. The various chapters and books of the Bible were written for very concrete situations. In order to understand what meaning the word holds for us, we need to think about the particular situations the author was addressing. Then we can ask what light this particular reading offers for our life and circumstances.

The purpose of this book is to provide background information to help us to understand the lectionary readings for Cycle B. It is intended to be used as the adult component of the series **Seasons of Faith.** Adults directing the family sessions outlined for **Seasons of Faith** will find useful background information for the discussions. In addition, adults in the family may find that the discussion questions proposed can provide a way of "Making God's Word My Own" in the family session. Adults using the series not only will find help in understanding the particular lectionary readings, but also in learning basic principles of biblical interpretation.

Some parishes may find this book useful for their catechumenate. Others may use it as part of an adult renewal program. Whether used in conjunction with the family sessions or alone, the book can be a helpful way of introducing Catholics to the Church's lectionary.

About the Authors

Irene Nowell, OSB, is associate professor and chair of the religious studies department at Benedictine College in Atchison, Kansas. She received her Ph.D. in Biblical Studies from the Catholic University of America in Washington, DC. She is the author of the *Commentary on Jonah, Tobit, and Judith* of the *Collegeville Bible Commentary* and the author of the article on Tobit and Nahum in the *New Jerome Biblical Commentary.* She was on the editorial team which produced the *Saint Andrew Bible Missal.* She is an associate editor of the journal, *The Bible Today,* and a frequent contributor to *Homily Service,* published by the Liturgical Conference.

Anne Marie Sweet, OSB, is a doctoral candidate in New Testament Studies at Notre Dame University. She is a frequent contributor to *Homily Service* and *Celebration.*

Jeanita F. Strathman Lapa is associate editor of **Seasons of Faith.** She holds a M.Ed. from Boston College and is an experienced religious educator.

Waiting on God

Readings: **Isaiah 63:16-17, 19, 64:2-7; 1 Corinthians 1:3-9; Mark 13:33-37**

Advent is a time for waiting. We reflect on all the waiting we do in our lives, and we see where God has been in the midst of our waiting. We enter into the spirit of the Israelites waiting for God to save them. We look forward to the time when, for each of us, all our waiting will be over, when God comes to take us to Himself. We look forward to the time when goodness will conquer the evil in our world. And we awaken ourselves to look for all the times when God comes to visit us in our daily lives.

The first reading for the First Sunday of Advent is from the last section of the book of the prophet Isaiah. This last section, chapters 56-66, was probably written during the difficult time of the Jews' return from exile in Babylon. Hopes had been high for a glorious return, but, in fact, poverty was widespread. There was dissension among the leaders. Rebuilding the ruins was an overwhelming task. The prophet who preaches to this community scolds them for their faint-heartedness. He challenges them to have courage and to persevere at their task of rebuilding. He continually reminds them that God will be faithful. God cares for them. With God's power they can be confident.

God is Father. God is also redeemer. (For the Hebrews, the *go'el,* your next of kin, was responsible for ransoming you in time of trouble.) God is Creator, the careful artist who shapes each person as the potter forms the pot (cf. Genesis 2:7). God is also powerful. The people plead for God to simply break through the heavens into their world (cf. Psalms 18, 68; Habakkuk 3). They declare that nowhere else is such a God known who does such wonders for a people (cf. Deuteronomy 4:6-8). They see God as in control of us, too. "Why do you **let us** wander . . . harden our hearts?" There is no claim that God should save the people because of their merit. They only hope that God should come and find them doing right. There is a strong sense of community. It is **all of us** who are sinners, and **all of us** hope for salvation from God for **all of us**.

We read the words from Isaiah as our own words as we await salvation from God. As we look at our own lives and at our world, we also recognize our need for God. Do we confidently expect God to save us, or have we begun to lose hope?

The second reading is taken from the introduction to Paul's First Letter to the Corinthians. The Corinthians were a very sophisticated, very enthusiastic people. In a city known for its licentiousness, they have embraced Christianity with gusto. They compete with one another for the most valued and evident signs of the Spirit.

Paul knows them. He repeatedly reminds them that they have been "called" (1:2, 9). He points out that their gifts of speech and knowledge, so important to them, are God's gifts in Christ Jesus. He also recognizes their other gifts, which he will discuss in chapters 12-14. But he points out that the most essential gift for their salvation is perseverance. God is faithful; God will sustain them as they wait. But they must wait to the end, remaining guiltless until the Day of the Lord.

We also await the Day of the Lord, the day when God will finally triumph, the day when Christ will come again, the day when we will meet God face to face.

The passage from the Gospel of Mark is the end of the apocalyptic discourse. The Gospel of Mark as a whole has a tone of apocalyptic eschatology. There is a great concern with events of the endtime. The end of the world is portrayed as a great cosmic catastrophe which results in the vindication of the just and the punishment of the wicked. Chapter 13 is a long speech of Jesus describing the tribulations and consequences of this cosmic catastrophe.

1

Two ideas are repeated in this section. First of all, no one but God knows the time of the end. Second, the proper response of the faithful disciple is to watch, to be ready at all times. Only those who persevere in watching will be saved.

Some people get caught up in interpreting the apocalyptic writings in such a way as to predict the time and the circumstances of the Day of the Lord. The usefulness of such an approach to one's Christian life is doubtful. The readings of our liturgy today take a different approach. The theme which runs through all these readings is that of waiting for God's salvation. God will come. We must be ready.

At Christmas we will celebrate the incarnation, God's coming as one of us, a baby born to Mary. Advent prepares us for that celebration. But Advent also calls us to be aware of all the other times God comes to us. We must be ready.

Irene Nowell, OSB

Questions for Discussion

1. Where do you see the need for God in our world today?

   Are their times when you have felt abandoned by God? When?

2. God is faithful and sustains us in our waiting. How do you experience this faithfulness in your life today?

3. What will it take for you to get ready to meet Christ at Christmas? In your everyday life? At the end of your life?

Questions for Journaling

Isaiah says of God, "We are the clay and you are the potter; we are all the work of your hands."

1. What does this mean to you?

2. How is this true in your life?

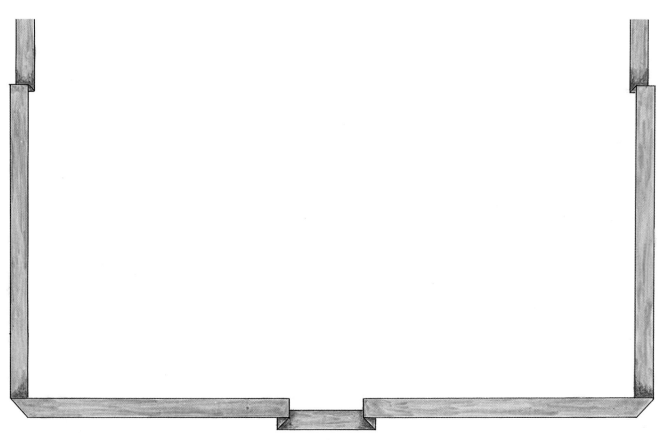

Prepare the Way of the Lord

Readings: **Isaiah 40:1-5, 9-11; 2 Peter 3:8-14; Mark 1:1-8**

As we look around our world, we see all around us the need for the Savior. We can see broken relationships that need to be healed in families and communities. We see poverty and injustice. We see hostilities between peoples and nations. We see the earth itself abused by people looking for selfish gain. Today we read about John the Baptist, who was sent to prepare the way for Jesus, the Messiah. We consider how each of us is called to prepare a way for the Lord this Advent. How can we prepare a way for the Lord in our world?

Most of us have at some time or another observed the building of a road. We have watched the huge tractors move piles of earth to fill in the low places and to make a smooth and level road. We have traveled on new roads which have eliminated the winding ways of the old roads. We understand the image of preparing a way, which Isaiah uses in the first reading.

The section of Isaiah chosen for this Sunday is one of the most familiar passages of the Old Testament. It is the beginning of the second section of the book, chapters 40-55, believed to have been written at the end of the Babylonian exile. (This opening passage resembles in some way the call of the anonymous prophet of the second section. There is a meeting with God, a commission, an objection, and reassurance. The selection for this Sunday omits the objection.)

The prophet is commissioned to give the exiled people new hope. He helps them to imagine their return from exile and the restoration of their land. The reassurance he proclaims is emphasized in the opening verses by the doubling of every announcement: "Comfort, comfort . . . speak tenderly, . . . service ended, iniquity pardoned." Why all this doubling? Israel has paid double for her sins.

The return will be a new exodus from a new slavery across a new desert. Like the exodus from Egypt, this new exodus from Babylon will reveal the glory of the Lord to all humankind (cf. Exodus 14:4). The sentinel who sees the approach of God leading the people is Zion (Jerusalem) herself. Perched on a high mountain, she sees the approach of the Lord. His arm is strong and gentle. He rules, but, like a shepherd, He gently gathers His lambs.

Can we imagine what it would be like if God were to rule in our world? How would it change our family? Our community? Our country?

The gospel is the beginning of the Gospel of Mark, the first to be written (c. A.D. 70) and the first to use the term *gospel* for a written work. Mark begins by stating his purpose: to tell the good news of Jesus who is the Christ (Messiah, Anointed One) and the Son of God. Both titles will be clouded by misunderstanding and secrecy until the end of the Gospel when Jesus answers "I am" to the high priest's question, "Are you the Christ?" (Mark 14:61-62), and when the centurion proclaims at Jesus' death, "Truly this was the Son of God" (Mark 15:39). Throughout this liturgical year, we will be reading primarily from the Gospel of Mark.

Mark begins his story of Jesus by introducing John the Baptist, whom he describes with phrases from Isaiah, Malachi, and Exodus (Exodus 23:20; Isaiah 40:3; Malachi 3:1). John is like the angel who prepares the way for God's people leaving Egypt in the exodus. John is like the prophet who proclaimed the return of God's people from exile in the new exodus. John is the messenger preparing for the day of the Lord, the great day of judgment when God's people will be vindicated.

John is also portrayed as Elijah, the great northern prophet of the ninth century B.C.E., who called Israel back to fidelity to Yahweh/God (cf. 1 Kings 17–2 Kings 1). John wears Elijah's clothes and eats Elijah's food. Elijah, who was taken up in a fiery chariot (2 Kings 1:12), was expected in Jewish tradition to return before the day of the Lord and/or the coming of the messiah (cf. Malachi 3:23). In modern Jewish tradition, a place is still set for Elijah at the Passover table, and a Passover song begs him to return and bring the messiah, the Son of David.

John, who is pictured with the images of every previous precursor of exodus and deliverance, preaches a baptism of repentance for the forgiveness of sins. He announces the arrival of one more powerful than he, who will baptize in the Spirit. John's preaching gives us a clue to how we can prepare our world for God's rule. Each of us must repent, change our ways, and live our lives guided by the Spirit.

The reading from 2 Peter also focuses on the arrival of the day of the Lord, the coming of the Messiah. The author, writing sometime in the second century A.D., gives a stern warning to those who have given up on the return of Christ. Some wonder why the second coming (the parousia) is delayed. They had expected the parousia immediately, and now they wondered if they had been deceived. The author points out that the reason for the delay is really God's patience with humankind who are not ready for judgment. He begs them to lead lives of such holiness that not only will they be ready for the day of the Lord, but that their goodness will hasten its coming. He assures them that the day will come. God does not work in human time. The new heavens and earth where God's justice will reside will arrive suddenly like a thief (Isaiah 65:17, 66:22; Revelation 21:1). Their task is to wait.

Because of Jesus Christ, our world is being transformed into a world where God reigns. Does Jesus Christ reign in my world? My family? My community? What do we need to do to prepare his way?

Irene Nowell, OSB

Questions for Discussion

1. What forms of abuse (e.g., abuse of people, land, self, alcohol, drugs) do you see in your town or your neighborhood? Where can hope be found?

2. What reassurance does this reading from Isaiah give you? How, when, do you feel the arms of the Lord encircling you?

3. What comfort do you find in the assurance that God is the ultimate ruler of the universe?

4. Today's readings call for change. What changes do you need to make in your life so that the kingdom of God may be furthered?

Questions for Journaling

Imagine a world where the justice of God reigns. What is the world like?

Or

Take time to reflect on the valleys (low times) and hills (times of joy and progress) in your life. Where are you in your journey to God?

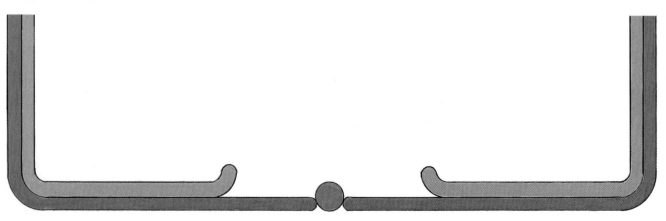

The Precursor

Readings: Isaiah 61:1-2, 10-11; 1 Thessalonians 5:16-24; John 1:6-8, 19-28

The third Sunday of Advent has traditionally been known as *Gaudete Sunday,* named for the first word of the reading from 1 Thessalonians as it reads in the Latin liturgy, *"Gaudete, iterim dico, gaudete. . . ."* "Rejoice, again I say, rejoice. . . ." Advent is a time to rejoice because the kingdom has begun. We, the Church, are called to be a sign of the kingdom, a glimpse of what it would be like if people lived with God at the center of their lives.

We look to Mary and the other saints as models for all of us in becoming this sign of the kingdom. Early in the Advent season, we celebrate the feast of St. Nicholas, whose gift giving inspires our own Christmas gift giving. We celebrate a feast day in honor of Mary, the first believer and model for the Church. Throughout the year we celebrate feast days of the saints, persons whose lives have been centered on God and who are signs for us of what it means to be filled with the Spirit of Jesus.

We return again in today's first reading to the third section of the Book of Isaiah, the section written shortly after the return from exile. The passage for this Sunday describes the call and anointing of the prophet. The vocabulary is similar to the Servant songs in Second Isaiah (Isaiah 42:1-4, 9:1-7, 50:4-11, 52:13-53:12). The connection between anointing and being filled with the Spirit of God is clearly made. (Compare the reading with the anointing of David in 1 Samuel 16.)

The prophet is given a commission of healing and liberation for God's people, who are discouraged with the struggle to restore the nation. The prophet proclaims a year of jubilee (cf. Leviticus 25:8-22) when debts are forgiven and land returns to its original owner. The question of ownership of land was a serious problem between those who returned from exile and those who remained behind.

In the last section, the prophet announces joy because God has clothed them in salvation and justice. God has made justice and praise spring up like a garden for all nations.

The theme of rejoicing continues in the reading from 1 Thessalonians. At the end of this letter Paul gives a whole series of directions to the faithful. He has just reminded them that the day of the Lord will come suddenly, like a thief in the night (5:2). They are to live in readiness by following these directions: always rejoice, pray, give thanks. They must test everything and encourage that which is good.

The author ends with a prayer that they may be kept whole by the God of peace. The Hebrew notion of peace (*shalom*) is the understanding that everything is in proper order and everyone has what is justly due for living. It is precisely the God of wholeness who will keep them whole. The Greek understanding is reflected in the notion that human beings are composed of spirit, soul, and body. All these components are to be kept whole for the day of the Lord. The faithful God calls them to this wholeness and will accomplish it within them.

In the Gospel of John, John the Baptist is portrayed as a witness. He testifies concerning his own identity and the identity of Jesus, who is the light. His testimony concerning himself is a negative testimony. Those with the authority to ask questions, the priests and Levites from Jerusalem, suggest three possibilities for his identity. Is he the messiah, the anointed king, like David, who will bring liberation, peace, and prosperity? Is he Elijah, the prophet who will come announcing the arrival of the day of the Lord? Is he a prophet like Moses, who will come to lead the people (cf. Deuteronomy 18:15-20)?

When they hear that he is none of these, they ask, "Who then are you?" Here, as in the other Gospels, the passage from Isaiah 40 is used to identify John. He prepares the way for the new exodus/return from exile. He prepares for the arrival of God the redeemer.

The interrogators have one more question: "Why then do you baptize?" Baptism was a form of initiation for Gentile converts to Judaism. The Essenes, a monastic-like sect of Judaism, also performed a baptismal rite as part of their initiation ceremonies in preparing for the Day of the Lord. John has many similarities to the Essenes and may have been one of them at one time. The question is: What is the purpose of John's baptism? John uses this opportunity to bear positive witness to the one who is to come, who will baptize, not in water, but in the Spirit.

The building of the kingdom is not something that human beings can accomplish on their own. The Church itself cannot build the kingdom. It is Jesus Christ, the real light, who works through the Church, which he fills with his Spirit. Our baptism is a sign of our repentance. It is a sign of our commitment to the kingdom. But all of this is possible because we are filled with God's Spirit. Because we are filled with God's Spirit, we rejoice.

Irene Nowell, OSB

Questions for Discussion

1. What has happened in this present season of Advent that gives you reason for rejoicing and thanksgiving?

2. Do you have "good news" today for the poor and oppressed peoples in our world? Will they hear what you have to say as "good news"? Why or why not?

3. Describe what God's kingdom of justice and peace would be like.

For Journaling

1. In times of fear and hopelessness I . . .

2. I rejoiced to see the Spirit at work this week when . . .

3. The model for my spiritual life is . . .

Saying Yes to God

Readings: 2 Samuel 7:1-5, 8-11, 16; Romans 16:25-27; Luke 1:26-38

On the Fourth Sunday of Advent we turn our thoughts to Mary, who is a model for the Christian believer. We read the story of the annunciation and ponder the fulfillment of God's promise through the "yes" of a young woman full of grace. Christians through the centuries have pondered this scene over and over as they repeat the angel Gabriel's words, "Hail, Mary, full of grace. . . ."

The story of the annunciation must be understood against the background of 2 Samuel 7, which is the foundation text for messianic hope. David, anointed king of Judah and Israel, is firmly in control of the nation, having established a capital and defeated enemies on all sides. He has brought the ark of the covenant to his capital city, making Jerusalem also the religious center. Now he wishes to build a temple, a house for the ark, and so he consults his court prophet, Nathan.

At first Nathan encourages David, but later he receives a message from the Lord which he relates to David. The essence of the message is: You will not build a house for me; I will build a house for you. The play on the word *house* (=temple=dynasty) carries the message. God, who called David from the sheepfold to be king, will establish his throne forever. His descendants, each anointed, will reign forever. (Remember, *messiah* is the Hebrew word for anointed; *Christ* is the Greek word for anointed.) David's heir will build the temple.

The first of these descendants, the first fulfillment of the messianic promise, is Solomon. It is Solmon who indeed builds the temple. But centuries pass and troubles beset the Davidic kingdom. Hope grows for another anointed one like David who will be the great king bringing peace and prosperity. But in 587 B.C.E., the kingdom falls to Babylon. The promise seems unfulfilled. But the messianic hope continues through the centuries, even though no Davidic heir sits on the throne again.

The annunciation story in the Gospel of Luke plays on many of the themes of 2 Samuel 7. In the Bible, there are accounts of the announcement of the birth of a number of persons: Samuel, Samson, John the Baptist, and Jesus, to name a few. Announcements of birth take on a standard form: (1) appearance of the Lord or an angel of the Lord, (2) fear or prostration on the part of the witness, (3) reassurance, (4) message concerning the birth of a son and his future, (5) objection by the recipient, (6) reassurance and often a sign (cf. Genesis 16:7-14, 17:15-21, 18:1-15; Judges 13:11-25). Both birth announcements in Luke follow this pattern: (1) 1:11, 1:26-28; (2) 1:12, 1:29; (3) 1:13, 1:30; (4) 1:13-17, 1:31-33; (5) 1:18, 1:24; (6) 1:19-20, 1:35-37.

In his message to Mary, Gabriel refers to many of the ideas from 2 Samuel 7. Jesus will be Son of the Most High (2 Samuel 7:14). He will have the throne of his father David (2 Samuel 7:12). He will reign forever (2 Samuel 7:13, 16). The evangelist presents Jesus as the fulfillment of the messianic hope.

The reading from Romans is the doxology (prayer of praise) with which the letter ends. It is a simple statement with many modifiers. The simple statement is: To God be glory forever, through Jesus Christ. Amen. On that simple statement are hung many of Paul's central ideas. The mystery of God's plan of long ago has now been revealed in Jesus Christ. That mystery is God's plan to save the world through Jesus' death and resurrection. An amazing part of the mystery is that even the Gentiles are to be saved through Christ. Faith in Christ is the way to this salvation. Both here and at the beginning of the letter (Romans 1:15), it is referred to as the "obedience of faith." God, who made and carried out this plan for our salvation, who alone is wise, is worthy of glory forever. Amen.

Catholics for centuries have sought to enter into the mystery of God's plan for our salvation by pondering the mystery with Mary. The "Hail Mary," the "Angelus," and the Rosary have been means of entering into the mystery of the incarnation. Mary is a central figure in our telling of the Christmas story in song, in drama, in art, and in celebration.

Irene Nowell, OSB

Questions for Discussion

1. What role does David play in the fulfillment of God's promise? What role does Mary play? What role do you play?

2. Mary says "yes" to God's call without knowing what it would mean. What have been similar times in your life?

3. How would your life have been different if you had said "no" instead? Would it have made a difference for anyone else?

4. How would Mary's life have been different if she had said "no"? What difference would it have made for others?

5. Each of us has a place in the unfolding story of our family history. How have you carried on the story of faith in your family?

For Journaling

For nine months Mary carried Christ within her. Imagine that you are visiting with Mary. Ask her what that pregnancy was like for her. Write what Mary tells you.

Holy Family

The Family of Jesus

Readings: **Sirach 3:2-6,12-14; Colossians 3:12-21; Luke 2:22-40**

The Feast of the Holy Family developed in the nineteenth century as part of the celebration of the Christmas season. The readings were chosen to emphasize the values of family life.

Ben Sira was a sage who lived in Jerusalem during the second century B.C.E. The Book of Sirach (called Ecclesiasticus in some versions of the Bible) is a collection of his teachings about the way to live wisely. One idea emphasized in the wisdom writings is the importance of honoring both father and mother. Both parents have equal authority over the children and have a right to expect obedience. In addition, adult children are obliged by the commandment to care for elderly parents. The care for elderly parents, in fact, is probably the original focus of the commandment.

Ben Sira emphasizes throughout his book that obeying God's commandments brings blessing and life, while disobeying God's commandments brings curse and death. In addition, the commandment concerning the honor due to parents is the only commandment to be listed with a reward, long life (cf. Exodus 20:12; Deuteronomy 5:16). Thus in chapter 3 we find the rewards of life, riches, forgiveness of sin, and answered prayer. Both obedience and care for elderly parents are mentioned.

The first section of the reading from the Letter to the Colossians (12-17) is a list of household virtues. This is a common form in the letters (cf. Romans 12:9-21; Ephesians 5:15-21). The virtues recommended apply to all human relationships. These are the virtues that keep the whole Christian family in peace, the virtues that allow Christians to live as one body. They should be as evident to other people as the clothes they wear.

Following this list of virtues is a series of exhortations to special groups: husbands and wives, parents and children, slaves and masters. The exhortation reflects the social situation of the time. It is presumed that even Christians will own slaves; it is presumed that even Christian husbands will have dominance over their wives. However, even in this social situation, the underlying principle is clear: each person should relate to the other with love, recognizing Christ's love as the perfect example.

Each year of the three-year cycle there is a different gospel. In Year A the gospel chosen from Matthew (2:13-15, 19-23) is the story of the flight into Egypt and the return. Joseph, modeled on the Joseph of Genesis who saved Israel's family (Genesis 37-50), takes his family to Egypt to escape the paranoia of Herod the Great, who killed any apparent threat to his throne. After Herod's death, Joseph brought the family back and settled them in the little town of Nazareth.

The other two cycles use stories from the Gospel of Luke. In Year B (2:22-40), we read the story of the family trip to the temple in Jerusalem in order to purify Mary after childbirth and to present the redemption for Jesus, a firstborn son (cf. Leviticus 12:2-8; Exodus 13:11-16). Two holy people meet the family in the temple: Simeon, who had been told by God that he would see the messiah before his death, and Anna, a prophet who spent all her time in the temple fasting and praying. Both people rejoice and proclaim the future greatness of the child.

In Year C we read the following story from Luke's Gospel, the story of the family's loss and subsequent finding of Jesus (2:41-52). The family has made its customary pilgrimage to Jerusalem for the Passover. On the return trip each parent thinks the twelve-year-old Jesus is with the other. Only at nightfall do they realize he is missing. For two more days they conduct an agonizing search in Jerusalem. Finally, on the third day, they find him discussing theology with the teachers in the temple. His cryptic answer to his mother's question, "I must be in my Father's house," puzzles both parents. However, they seem to return to a normal life in Nazareth.

9

All three of these gospel stories foreshadow the passion. Jesus will be tried and convicted on the charge of claiming to be Messiah; over his head the charge will read, "King of the Jews." He will indeed be the sign of contradiction seen by Simeon; he himself will be the firstborn who pays the ransom for all God's children. Finally, he will be lost for three days, but will again be found about his Father's business. Even the quiet family life foreshadows the future.

Irene Nowell, OSB

Questions for Discussion

1. What are ways you honor your parents today? Do we as Christians have any responsibility for elderly people in our parish whose children live far away?

2. Sirach wrote instructions for sons and daughters, outlining their responsibilities to their parents. Paul explained to first-century Christians how their faith should transform their family life. What advice might the wise person have for modern families? How should faith transform our family life?

For Journaling

1. What my family needs most right now is . . .

2. What I have to give to my family now is . . .

3. What do you find difficult about this responsibility? In what way is it a blessing?

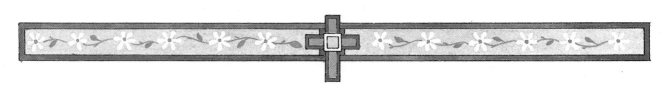

Christmastide

Readings: Isaiah 60:1–6; Ephesians 3:2–3, 5–6; Matthew 2:1–12

The Feast of Epiphany is a feast for all nations. The word *epiphany* means manifestation. The Epiphany celebrates the manifestation to all peoples of God's good news in Christ.

The first reading is from the final section of the Book of Isaiah, called Trito-Isaiah. This final section (chapters 56–66) is a collection of prophetic oracles criticizing the current leadership of God's people (sixth century B.C.E.) and looking forward to a day when faithful people of all nations will worship God in sincerity. At the center of this collection is a vision of the new Jerusalem, home of God's faithful people.

One predominant image throughout the final section of Isaiah is the image of light. In today's reading the new Jerusalem is described in terms of light. God's glory has come to shine upon the city. Because of God's light, Jerusalem itself becomes light, while all other nations languish in darkness. Thus all other nations will walk by Jerusalem's light, the glory of God within it. All these nations will then bring tribute in gratitude to God's house in Jerusalem. They will bring their most precious treasures, gold, frankincense, and silver, along with flocks of animals for sacrifice. Jerusalem will be a holy city, forever enlightened by the presence of God.

The reading from the Letter to the Ephesians describes specifically God's plan in Christ for the Gentiles. Paul was appointed as special minister of the gospel to the Gentiles. The letter points out that people in former ages did not understand that God's mercy extended to all peoples. The good news in Christ is that the Gentiles now share in the salvation offered in past ages to the Jews. Now the Gentiles share in the covenant promises. Now the Gentiles are equal heirs of Abraham. Now Gentiles and Jews are even one body in Christ! This is indeed good news.

The gospel story gives the focus to the feast. Matthew's story of the astrologers points out at the beginning of his Gospel that Gentile wise men recognize Jesus as Messiah even when Jerusalem teachers do not. Gentile wise men worship the child; Judah's king fears him.

Wise men arrive from the east, probably Mesopotamia where astrology and astronomy were well developed. They have seen a special star which indicates the birth of a king. Such astronomical events were frequently associated with special events. They have arrived bearing gifts for the royal child. Herod the Great, however, defended his throne with paranoid jealousy. In the course of his reign he killed his favorite wife, as well as a brother-in-law and children who had a better claim to the throne than he did. He does not welcome the search of the magi for "the King of the Jews," and plots to kill the child when he is found.

The official priests and scribes quote the messianic prophecies which identify Bethlehem, the city of David's birth, as the birthplace of the messiah. Apparently, however, they do not follow their own wisdom. Only the Gentile wise men seek the child to offer their gifts. This child will bring the good news: now the Gentiles are equal heirs of God's promises.

Irene Nowell, OSB

Questions for Discussion

1. There are some people who are devoted to God, but do not belong to the Church. There are some people who belong to the Church, but are not devoted to God. Do you agree? Why or why not?

2. What do you think keeps some people who are seeking God from coming to the Church?

3. What should be our attitude toward these people?

4. Why do you think some people who belong to the Church never find a personal faith and relationship with God?

For Journaling

1. I seek God by . . .

2. My first experience of personal faith was . . .

Baptism of the Lord

Here Is My Chosen One

Readings: Isaiah 42:1-4, 6-7; Acts 10:34-38; Mark 1:7-11

With this Sunday, the Christmas season ends. Our contemplation of the mystery of Jesus' birth and early life concludes with the story of his baptism, his call to his specific mission. The baptism opens the story of his public life, his following of the call which will end only with his death and resurrection.

The three gospel stories of Jesus' baptism are read in Years A (Matthew 3:13-17), B (Mark 1:7-11), and C (Luke 3:15-16, 21-22). There are some common elements and some differences in emphasis. Common to all the narratives are the basic incidents. Jesus comes to the Jordan where John is baptizing. John baptizes Jesus. After Jesus is baptized, the sky opens, a voice is heard proclaiming him beloved son, the Spirit descends in the form of a dove.

Baptism was an initiation rite practiced by some Jewish sects, especially the Essenes. It symbolized cleansing and entrance into new life. The Gospels interpret John's baptism as a baptism of repentance. The images surrounding Jesus' baptism suggest the exodus and creation. Wind (spirit) and water are primary images at both events. The creative, naming voice of God recalls the word of God at creation naming every creature. Jesus, the beloved son, recalls Israel at the exodus being named Yahweh's firstborn (Exodus 4:22).

In Matthew, John protests his unworthiness to baptize Jesus. Matthew's audience probably included some former followers of John. The Gospel emphasizes that Jesus is superior to John and that he acts in "righteousness," one of Matthew's favorite words. Mark is characteristically brief. His description of the sky "rent in two" recalls the prayer of the returned exiles in the sixth century (Isaiah 63:19), that God would rend the sky in two and deliver them again as in the exodus. Luke emphasizes Jesus' prayer, just as he does at all the significant moments in Jesus' life.

In all the Gospels, Jesus is publicly proclaimed God's Son at his baptism. He is filled with the Spirit. From that moment on, he begins his lifework of proclaiming the kingdom of God.

The proclamation of Jesus as God's beloved son is phrased in the words of Second Isaiah. There are four songs in the work of this sixth-century prophet (Isaiah 40-55) which describe a servant of the Lord. This passage is the first of the four songs. The servant is described as a chosen one in God's favor, filled with God's spirit. The task of the servant is to bring God's righteousness to all the nations. The servant will himself become the covenant, the bond between God and the people. As he brings God's justice, the servant will liberate those enslaved by darkness. Later songs will reveal the cost of this mission to the servant. He will suffer for the sins of many; his suffering will bring them life. (See especially Isaiah 52:13-53:12.)

The early Church found this figure of the servant a way to explain the mission of Jesus. From the call at his baptism to the description of his death, the Gospels use images from the four servant songs.

The second reading is part of Peter's speech to the Gentile Cornelius. In telling the good news, Peter begins the story of Jesus with his baptism. The baptism is Jesus' call and commission to begin the work of our salvation. That work culminates in Jesus' death and resurrection. Our entrance into the new life won for us by Jesus is through baptism into his death and anointing by the Holy Spirit. That is our exodus, our deliverance from sin. That is our new creation. That is our commissioning to continue the work of Jesus in the world.

Irene Nowell, OSB

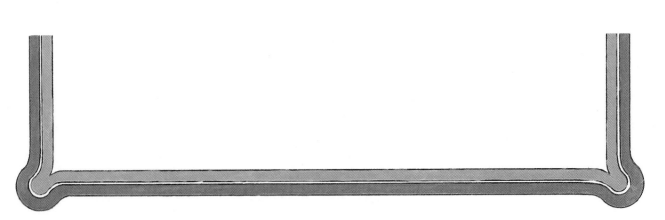

Questions for Discussion

1. The Christmas season has come to a close. What was special about this Christmas for you? What was the best gift you received? Why do you value that gift most?

2. At his baptism Jesus was publicly proclaimed God's Son and then "filled with the Spirit." From that moment on, he began his life work of proclaiming the kingdom of God. At our baptism we too were filled with the Spirit. How are we called to proclaim the kingdom of God? How is God present with us in our mission?

3. Jesus turned to prayer before any significant event in his life. How has prayer helped you to make the important decisions in your life?

Question for Journaling

When we give someone a name, we establish a special relationship with that person. The "creative voice of God" calls Jesus "beloved son." At our baptism God also called and named each one of us as His daughter or son. How does it feel to be called and named by God?

God Calls—I Respond

Readings: **1 Samuel 3:3-10, 19; 1 Corinthians 6:13-15, 17-20; John 1:35-42**

In our lives we are called to many things, small and great. We are called to supper, called to serve on committees or a jury, called to our life's work, called to our lifelong relationships with other people. This Sunday's readings are about call, especially the significant calls in our lives.

The reading from 1 Samuel tells the story of the call of Samuel. The tradition has already indicated that Samuel is an important person in the story of God's dealing with His people. Samuel is born in answer to prayer and is dedicated to God at an early age. For this reason, he is living with Eli, the priest who serves the ark of the covenant, and with his sons.

The ark of the covenant was for the Israelites the sign of the presence of God. There was at this time no established central sanctuary where everyone was to come to worship. Jerusalem was still in the hands of the Jebusites. So, wherever the ark was, that place was the center for worship. When Samuel was young, the ark was at Shiloh.

There was also no king or central ruler for all the tribes. Local judges arose from time to time to take action against enemies, but no one of the stature of Moses or Joshua had emerged. The priest serving the ark was thus one of the most influential men of the community. But Eli was weak and his sons were wicked. Thus there was a vacuum in leadership.

Out of this context God calls the young Samuel. Samuel is willing to listen, but he does not know who is calling him. Even though Eli is weak, he understands the workings of God. He knows that it is God who calls Samuel. He also instructs the boy in the proper way to respond to the call of God: "Speak, Lord, your servant is listening." Samuel follows Eli's direction and responds to God's call. His first message from the Lord is that the house of Eli has been rejected. As he grows in God's service, Samuel himself will be a major leader of the people and will be instrumental in anointing the first two of Israel's kings, Saul and David. It is a significant task to which God calls young Samuel.

The gospel reading is the Johannine version of Jesus' call of the disciples. John the Baptist announces Jesus and describes him as "Lamb of God." The image of lamb would have recalled two passages from the Hebrew Scriptures or Old Testament. The primary allusion is, of course, to the lamb slaughtered at Passover whose blood on the doorpost saves the Israelites from the angel of death (cf. Exodus 12:13, 23). The image of the lamb led to slaughter is also used in the last part of the Book of Isaiah to describe the Servant of God (Isaiah 53:7). The evangelists use both of these passages to help describe Jesus' passion. John uses the image here as his introduction to Jesus.

Naming is important in this first part of John's Gospel. The Baptist names Jesus "Lamb of God." The two disciples who follow Jesus name him "rabbi," which means "great one" or "teacher." After spending the afternoon with Jesus, Andrew names him "messiah," which means "anointed." The anointed one would be king or priest. Andrew brings his brother Simon to Jesus, and Jesus gives Simon the name "Cephas," which in Aramaic means "rock." The Greek version of the same name is "Peter."

Names in any culture indicate the character of the person who bears them. In the Hebrew culture naming also had a creative power. Naming someone created that person. To have someone's name (which was in a sense that person's identity) was to have a certain power over that person. We recognize that in our use of names when we give special people special names or when we say to someone, "May I use your name (= your influence)?"

The second reading begins a series of readings from Paul's First Letter to the Corinthians. During this season of the year, the second reading is not chosen specifically to have the same theme as the gospel and first reading. The second reading is generally part of a series from one of the New Testament letters. Such is the case on this Sunday. The First letter to the Corinthians will be read from this Sunday through the Sixth Sunday of the Year. That is why Paul's discussion of the dignity of the human body and of sexuality does not relate to the prevailing theme of call on this Sunday. Paul's message, however, was essential for those who lived in Corinth, a city where sexual excess was frequent and everywhere. It is an important message for us, too.

Irene Nowell, OSB

Questions for Discussion

1. Each of us is called by God in the particular circumstances of our own lives. In what way does God call you through your family? Your job or profession? Your civic community? Your parish? Your gifts and talents? Your baptism?

2. The ark of the covenant was for the Israelites the sign of the presence of God. Later the temple became the sign of God's presence. Paul says **our body** is the temple of God, the temple of the Holy Spirit. We are a place where God abides. What difference does this make in our lives?

For Journaling

1. When God looks at me, He sees . . .

2. When others look at me, they see . . .

3. God is calling me . . .

Faith in Jesus Changes Our Lives

Readings: **Jonah 3:1-5, 10; 1 Corinthians 7:29-31; Mark 1:14-20**

The readings this Sunday call us to conversion, to a radical change in our lives because of God's call. We often fail to expect it of ourselves.

The Book of Jonah is a wonderful story told to illustrate the power of God's mercy and the possibility of change for the better, even in those we consider most wicked. Jonah was sent by God to the city of Nineveh to preach to the people there. Nineveh was the capital of Assyria, Israel's most hated enemy. The Assyrians took over many countries in their sweep toward world empire, and they were terribly cruel to the people they conquered. Eventually in 622 B.C.E., they conquered the northern kingdom of Israel itself and took the people into captivity. Thus Nineveh, the Assyrian capital, became the symbol of the evil empire.

Jonah did not want to go to Nineveh. Jonah did not want the Ninevites to be converted and forgiven by God. He thought God belonged only to the Israelites, and only they should enjoy God's mercy. Jonah made one attempt to flee from God's call. Today's reading begins with God's repetition of the call. To Jonah's amazement and chagrin, as soon as he begins to preach to the Ninevites, they repent and turn to God for mercy. In this they are much more docile than the Israelites who ignored more than one prophetic call to repentance.

The consequence of the Ninevites' repentance, however, was no surprise to Jonah. He already knew God was merciful, and in chapter 4 of the book he complains to God about His forgiving ways. Thus it is no surprise to Jonah that as soon as the Ninevites give evidence of repentance, God immediately repents of the punishment He had intended to inflict. Jonah knew what is evident in the Old Testament: God is gracious and merciful and forgiving. In fact the verb *repent* is used much more often of God than of human beings in the Old Testament. That was the way they understood God.

The Book of Jonah is not a prophetic work; it is a fictional story. It is written to tell a profound truth to the people of the time and to us. The book was written sometime around the fourth century B.C.E. At that time the Jews, who had returned from the Babylonian exile, had developed some very strict rules about association with Gentiles. They were afraid that these non-Jews would lead them away from God. But, in separating themselves, they were in danger of forgetting that God is the God of all people and that God calls even the Gentiles to repentance and forgiveness. The Book of Jonah was written to emphasize that truth.

In the gospel reading Jesus makes a similar proclamation. The kingdom of God is at hand; repent and believe the good news. The Gospel of Mark, which will be read throughout Cycle B, is the shortest of all the Gospels. This announcement of Jesus' preaching is told with customary brevity. Jesus announces the call to conversion and to faith in God's good news of forgiveness and new life. The effect of Jesus' preaching is seen in the call of the first disciples. They follow "immediately" (one of Mark's favorite words).

The same sense of immediacy is found in the continued reading from 1 Corinthians. Paul is expecting the second coming of Jesus at any moment. He is telling believers that the only important thing is faith in Jesus. All other things are passing away. Paul was mistaken about the time of Jesus' second coming. It did not happen immediately. But he was not mistaken in his sense of priority. Life in Jesus is the one important thing. All other things are subordinate to that one thing.

Have you ever experienced one moment that changed your whole life? It is that sort of change these readings are describing. Each reading portrays the call to turn completely to God with no holding back. That is radical conversion.

Irene Nowell, OSB

Questions for Discussion

1. As changes come to our political world, we are at times appropriately wary. "Is this change in policy in good faith?" we wonder. When does our natural wariness turn to refusal to let people change? How do we get locked into our own judgments? Does this ever happen in our personal lives?

2. Christians are called to help further God's kingdom. Are there times when you feel overwhelmed with this task? What gives you courage?

3. Jonah was sent to the Ninevites to call them to repentance. God sends us to the world to call it to repentance. How can we give that message? Are there things we do to obscure the call?

For Journaling

1. I feel like Jonah when . . .

2. Conversion to me means . . .

3. When I feel like running away . . .

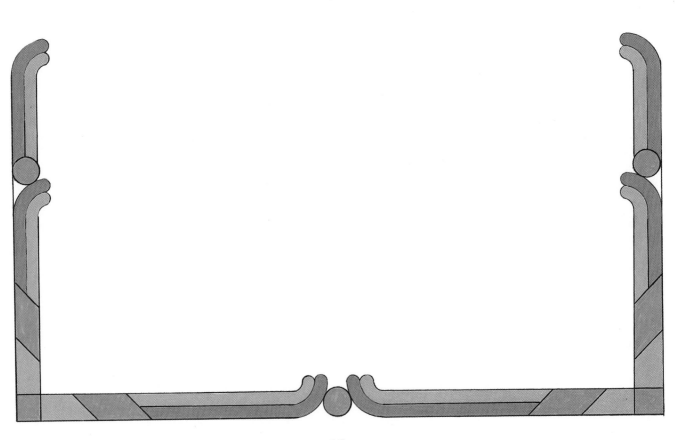

Fourth Sunday in
Ordinary Time

God Reveals Himself to Us through Jesus

Readings: Deuteronomy 18:15-20; 1 Corinthians 7:32-35; Mark 1:21-28

In our lives we are always in need of people who speak with authority in areas that are important to us. One important area is the word of God. How do we know who has the authority to tell us the will of God? How do we know whom to believe? Throughout biblical times people asked these same questions. Today's readings deal with some of the answers.

The Book of Deuteronomy is a retelling of the story of Moses and the Israelites in the desert. The author told the story again for the people of the seventh century B.C.E., who were faced with threats from major foreign powers. The prophet Jeremiah preached at about the same time. Both were convinced of the urgency of the situation and tried to convince the people to abandon their evil ways and to follow God's ways. To continue in sin would mean certain defeat and exile (which did in fact happen in 587 B.C.E.). It was, therefore, very important to know which prophets to listen to, which authority to obey.

The Book of Deuteronomy presents Moses' solution to the problem. In the desert the people had listened to Moses; Moses was the person who conveyed God's word to them. Thus Moses was a true prophet. The promise of God delivered by Moses is that another prophet will be raised up by God to tell the people God's word. The true prophet will deliver God's word. The false prophet delivers his own message. The test of the prophet is the fulfillment of his word, not a very easy thing for his contemporaries to judge. The punishment for false prophecy is death.

This message concerning the prophet may not seem to be very helpful. Only by attempting to discern whether the prophet's message comes from God can the people tell if a prophet is true. But this passage became very important in the last centuries before Christ. One of the figures whom people began to await to deliver them from their present misery was "a prophet like Moses." The Qumran community who lived by the Dead Sea expected a prophet, a priest, and a kingly messiah. In the Gospel of John, the Pharisees ask John the Baptist if he is "the prophet" (cf. John 1:25). This image of the prophet is dependent on this passage from Deuteronomy.

Christians see Jesus as the true prophet, the one who not only brings the word of God, but who is the Word of God. In the first chapter of the Gospel of Mark, there are several stories illustrating Jesus' authority. The passage chosen for today tells of Jesus casting out a demon. The people are amazed because the demon obeys him. Where can his authority come from?

A second example of Jesus' authority may seem less spectacular, but is nonetheless significant. Jesus teaches with authority, more authority than the established religious leaders of his day. He teaches as if he brings the authentic word of God. The people listening to him believe that he has the authority to tell them God's word. The people judge Jesus to be a true prophet, a true messenger of God.

After Jesus' resurrection the problem remains with the Church: How do we know the true word of God, the true messenger of God? Some of the early Christian communities found Paul to be a true prophet. The Christians at Corinth apparently wrote to Paul, asking him a whole series of practical questions about how to live the Christian life. The First Letter to the Corinthians is Paul's answer to their questions. In today's passage he is again proclaiming that devotion to God is the one thing necessary. Any other aspect of human life, even marriage, is secondary to wholehearted dedication to God. That is the heart of Paul's word from God.

19

How do we know today who brings the authentic word of God? We know that the magisterium speaks with God's authority. But how do we test our prophets? How do we know whom to accept? These were not easy questions for the Israelites or for the early Christians. Neither are they easy questions for us.

Irene Nowell, OSB

Questions for Discussion

1. How can we determine who has the authority to speak in the name of Jesus? What criteria can guide us?

2. What helps you to keep your focus on God? Does anything in your daily life tend to keep you from loving God with your whole being?

3. How does your family help you to keep your focus on God?

For Journaling

1. I am called to be a prophet by . . .

2. I feel divided when . . .

Presented to the Lord

Readings: **Malachi 3:1–4; Hebrews 2:14–18; Luke 2:22–40**

Presenting a new baby to family and friends is a joyous occasion. Family and friends gather for baby showers or come to visit to see the new baby. Brothers and sisters, grandparents, aunts and uncles, all wait for a chance to hold the new baby. Holding the new baby is a graced moment, full of the wonder of life and of hope for the future. Proud parents also present their child to the Church to meet the Lord present in the community of faith. In this new baby the community also meets the Lord, the author of life.

Mary and Joseph also brought their child to the temple to meet their community of faith. Today's feast celebrates that meeting. The feast was first celebrated in the Church in Jerusalem in the late fourth century. It was known as *Hipopante,* the Feast of Meeting. Since then, the feast has had several different titles, the Meeting of Jesus and Simeon, the Purification of Mary, and the Presentation of the Lord. In the 1960 revision of the Roman calendar, the Church chose to return to the older tradition and celebrate today as a feast of the Lord.

Forty days after his birth, following the Jewish custom, Jesus is brought to the temple and presented to God. Here he meets Simeon and Anna who represent all the believing people who have long awaited this day. Mary and Joseph present their infant son to God as the Law of Moses prescribed: "Consecrate to me every firstborn that opens the womb . . ." (Exodus 13:2).

Jesus' parents brought with them " 'a pair of turtledoves and two young pigeons' in accord with the dictates of the laws of the Lord." According to Jewish law, the parents of the firstborn were to redeem their son by the prescribed sacrifice. The firstborn son was understood to belong to God, and the parents had to redeem the child by offering a sacrifice.

The temple was for the people of Israel the place where God dwelled. It is here that Jesus meets Simeon and Anna. Simeon, a just and pious man who has been awaiting the "consolation of Israel," is filled with hope as he takes the child Jesus in his arms. In Simeon the chosen people welcome Jesus as the long-awaited one who would fulfill the promise of God, the one who would deliver Israel from its long period of oppression. Here is the one who would be the "glory of Israel and revealing light to the Gentiles" (Luke 2:30–32). Simeon also reveals to the amazed parents that not all people would rejoice in his birth. Their son will also face great suffering. Now there is joy, but later there would be great grief for his mother and for many others. In this story Anna, a widow, a woman, not a "son of the covenant," represents the poor, the marginalized, the outsiders, who also find in this child their hope.

In the first reading, the prophet Malachi confronts the temple priests with their infidelity. There will be a time of reckoning. Someday God's messenger will purify the temple and its priesthood. Then there will be true worship in God's temple.

Luke's story of the presentation of Jesus in the temple as a child recalls this prophecy. After Jesus' death and resurrection, the followers of Jesus used this reading from Malachi to describe the significance of this event. Malachi was a prophet who tried to reanimate the faith of the people of his times by reminding them of their hope of a messiah. The followers of Jesus retell the story to reanimate the faith of the people in Jesus, the fulfillment of God's promise. Jesus is presented as the trustworthy priest who continues to act on their behalf. Jesus is seen as the anointed one, God's Son who brought about a new kingdom in their midst. Jesus as the high priest offered his sacrifice once and for all. His sacrifice was the sacrifice of his self, his whole life given so that we might be with our God forever.

Throughout the season of Advent and throughout the Christmas season, our thoughts have been centered on the coming of Jesus, the fulfillment of the messianic promise. Every year we celebrate this event in the story of our salvation. Yet, as we look around our world and even at our own lives, we know that salvation is not complete. Jesus has left his followers with the task of announcing the good news of salvation. We are to be a sign of God's kingdom, God's reign. Through his followers Jesus reaches out to the many who need comfort and healing. In a sense, we are the further fulfillment of the promise as we bring aid and comfort to the sick, the oppressed, the hungry. We continue this story of hope as we extend the gift of compassion to all our brothers and sisters everywhere. Through us the light of Jesus shines.

This day has traditionally been celebrated with a procession with lighted candles. Occasionally you will hear someone call this Candlemas Day. The procession with lighted candles re-enacts a welcoming parade. The true light of the world is welcomed into the temple. We welcome the light of the world into our lives. Today we bless candles and pray that we who carry them will "walk in the path of goodness and come to the light that shines forever." For centuries Catholics have taken some of these blessed candles home. In times of trouble or danger, they light the candle to remind themselves that the light of Christ is with them always. The lighted candle is a sign of God's presence and protection, a sign of the power of the risen Lord in our homes.

Jeanita Strathman Lapa

Questions for Discussion

1. Recall the look in the eyes of a grandparent who is presented and holds the first grandchild. What does this look reveal?

2. What hopes and dreams does this feast rekindle in you?

3. What light can you bring to your family today?

4. What hopes for the world can be fulfilled only in you?

For Journaling

1. I am a light for the world when . . .

2. What gives me hope is . . .

Fifth Sunday in
Ordinary Time

The Lord Loves the Oppressed

Readings: Job 7:1-4, 6-7; 1 Corinthians 9:16-19, 22-23; Mark 1:29-39

What is the meaning of suffering? That problem has preoccupied people throughout the ages. There seems to be no explanation that completely satisfies the human mind. The Book of Deuteronomy proposed one way to deal with the problem of suffering: suffering is punishment for sin. If you are obedient to God, you will be blessed. If you are disobedient, you will be punished.

Centuries after the Book of Deuteronomy was written, the theory was distorted and reversed in the ever-present search to be able to judge one another. The reversed version runs something like this: If you are suffering, you must have sinned; if you are prosperous, you must be holy. The theory is still very much alive in our minds today. If something painful happens to us (or even something wonderful), we ask: What did I do to deserve this?

Even in the earliest times, however, people knew the theory didn't work. They knew that good people suffered and wicked people prospered (cf. Psalms 37 and 73). The Book of Job is one attempt to deal with the failure of the theory. Job is a holy and righteous man. In order to test him to see if he is righteous only for the sake of the reward (if you are virtuous, you will be blessed), God allows Satan to inflict all kinds of suffering on Job. Job recognizes that his situation is not according to the theory. This is the basis of all of his complaints to God throughout the book. His friends, however, who come to "comfort" him, cannot imagine any other reality than the theory. They insist to the end that Job must have sinned. Otherwise, why would he be suffering? All he needs to do is repent, and God will remove the punishment from him.

There are some interesting things to note about the book. The friends, who are so sure they understand all God's ways, never speak to God. Even though he suspects that God is the cause of his troubles, Job will not let go of God. He demands from God an account of the situation. He demands a face-to-face encounter. God not only answers Job, he declares that Job is the one who has spoken rightly, not the friends. At the conclusion Job is granted twice as much wealth as he had before. And God has won the wager with Satan: Job was faithful, not for the sake of the reward, but for God. But the theory also stands: God rewards Job's fidelity.

The idea that suffering is related to sin and evil is not wrong. It is only the specific equation between one person's sin and the same person's suffering that does not always hold true in the plan of God. The stories of Jesus' miracles, however, deal specifically with the relationship between suffering and evil. Jesus' miracles are a sign of God's presence and power working within Jesus. Specifically, they are a sign that the power of Satan is broken and the kingdom of God has arrived. If the power of Satan is broken, then the power of all evil is broken. The arrival of the kingdom of God means the breaking of the power of sin, death, sickness, pain, alienation, war, poverty, and all other signs of evil.

Mark continues his description of Jesus' authority by showing his power over evil. In today's passage Jesus heals those who are sick and those possessed by demons, by evil. The power by which he does this is the power of God. Through prayer he maintains his constant communion with the Father, source of his power. Besides defeating the power of evil, he proclaims the other side of the same truth: If the power of Satan is broken, the kingdom of God has arrived. That is the good news.

23

Several times in his letters, Paul defends his ministry. In this section of 1 Corinthians he declares that the preaching of the good news is not something he does by choice. The good news of Jesus is so powerful that he is compelled to proclaim it. The good news has taken possession of him.

Have you ever said, "Why do I deserve this?" Do you wonder why the innocent suffer? Do you believe that Jesus has really broken the power of evil and that the kingdom of God has arrived? What is our mission as Christians in terms of continuing Jesus' mission against evil and suffering, continuing his proclamation of the good news? How can you reconcile the fact that Jesus suffered with the news that the power of evil is broken?

Irene Nowell, OSB

Questions for Discussion

1. When children grow up in an abusive home, they often grow up to be adults who are abusive to their children. How can this cycle of evil be broken?

2. How does our abuse of the environment and the earth affect the children of the next century? What is our responsibility for ending the cycle of abuse of the environment and the earth?

3. How can you reconcile the fact that Jesus suffered with the news that the power of evil is broken?

For Journaling

1. I can begin to change the force of evil by . . .

2. Because Jesus has broken the power of evil . . .

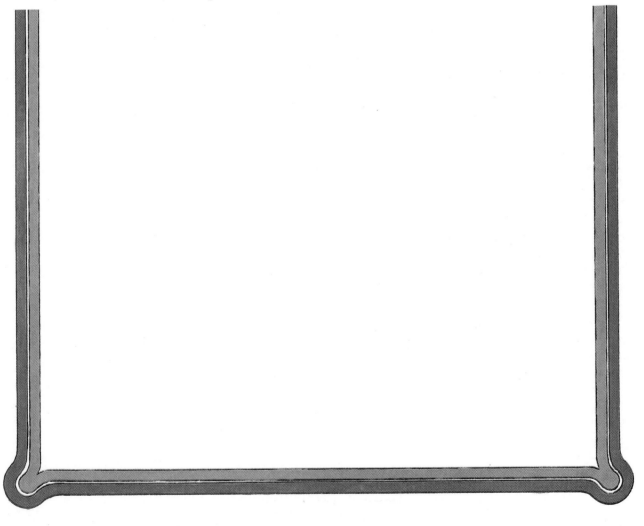

Jesus Cares, We Care

Readings: **Leviticus 13:1-2, 44-46; 1 Corinthians 10:31-11:1; Mark 1:40-45**

The belief that Jesus has broken the power of evil, which was discussed last Sunday, has a real effect on the way we treat people who are suffering. Our normal instinct is to avoid suffering at all costs. Our call to continue the ministry of Jesus calls us to confront evil and to touch and heal the suffering wherever we can.

The Book of Leviticus is a collection of Hebrew or Old Testament law codes. Many of the laws have to do with proper worship of God. Some of those laws restricted which people were permitted to offer public worship to God. Those who were considered worthy to offer worship were declared "clean." Those who were unworthy for some reason were declared "unclean." Usually being "unclean" had nothing to do with moral guilt. More often it referred to some bodily imperfection which was thought to make one unable to approach God. Physical mutilation, the flow of bodily fluids, contact with a dead body, all these things made a person unclean. Skin diseases of any kind also made a person unclean. Because little was known about the process of contagion, the person with any skin disease was also banished from the community as long as the disease lasted. Thus such a person was cut off from worship of God and also cut off from normal community life. Such excommunication was a terrible thing. The outcasts were among the most miserable in Israelite society. They became a living symbol of the effect of sin.

The gospel story continues the account of Jesus' authority over evil. Not only does he have power to cure disease, he also has power to heal the separation from the community and the separation from God which leprosy signified. It is only a small step from the healing of leprosy to the forgiveness of sin. In the next chapter of Mark's Gospel, we find Jesus declaring that he is able to forgive sin. He does forgive sinners.

Jesus' approach to the leper scandalized the people of his time. Not only does he speak to the outcast, he touches him. By touching a leper, Jesus has also rendered himself unclean. According to the law, Jesus is now unable to offer public worship until he himself is purified. Jesus disregards the law and, in so doing, demonstrates again that the kingdom of God has arrived, the power of Satan is broken.

Another phrase which should be noted in the gospel story is Jesus' instruction to the leper to tell no one of the event. That admonition is given by Jesus in almost every miracle story. It is usually disregarded by the person who has been cured. What is the purpose of the instruction? Why does Jesus command people not to tell the miracle? Scholars have discovered that this instruction occurs most often in the Gospel of Mark. They believe that it is emphasized by Mark as a special part of his message. Mark shows Jesus avoiding the title of "messiah" and any claim to be a "wonder-worker."

Even the disciples are instructed not to tell about such events as the transfiguration. It is as if it were a secret that Jesus is the Messiah. The secret is broken only after his death. Only after they witness Jesus' suffering and death and experience his resurrection can the disciples know what it means to be "messiah." Only then will they know what it means that Jesus has broken the power of sin and death, and that the kingdom of God has arrived. Until then they cannot tell the secret because they do not know its meaning.

The short passage from 1 Corinthians refers to a problem the early Christians had concerning meat sold in the market. Often such meat had been offered to idols. Yet it was impossible to know about particular meat. Some Christians with tender consciences refused to eat meat at all. Others, declaring that God made all things holy, ate any meat with abandon. Paul's advice is to avoid scandalizing one another at all costs. Meat was not the question. Offending a fellow Christian was.

Jesus was open to all people, even those excommunicated by established religious authorities. It is very difficult to imitate his compassion and his freedom. Yet, if we believe that he has broken the power of evil, how can we do otherwise?

Irene Nowell, OSB

Questions for Discussion

1. Who are the outcasts in our community? Why are they considered outcasts? What should be a Christian's approach to them?

2. What are some things that give scandal in our community? When is it important to avoid offending other members of the community?

3. What does our parish do to reach out to those affected by sin or suffering?

For Journaling

1. I find it difficult to imitate Jesus' compassion when . . .

2. I find it difficult to imitate Jesus' freedom when . . .

3. Jesus reached out and touched me when . . .

Jesus Heals through the Sacraments

Readings: **Isaiah 43:18-19, 21-22, 24-25; 1 Corinthians 1:18-22; Mark 2:1-12**

The stories of Jesus' authority over evil and suffering continue in the gospel readings. People find it easier to believe in the healings they can see. It is vitally important to believe also in the unseen healings. Often they are even more important.

The first reading is from Second Isaiah, the section written just as the people were beginning to return from the Babylonian exile. One characteristic of this section is the repeated statement by God of being present and having the power to save. The people in exile had grown discouraged about the possibility of return. They wondered if Yahweh had abandoned them. Throughout Second Isaiah (chapters 40-55), God reassures the people: "I, it is I. I am the one who saves." It is not God who has burdened the people; it is the people who have burdened God with their sins. God will remove the burden, will wipe away their sins.

Consistent images throughout Second Isaiah are the new exodus and new creation. God who was able to save them from Egypt; God, who created the world, will be able to save them from Babylon and create them as a new people. God led them home through the desert once before; God can and will do it again. God created a people once before from an old man and a barren woman; God can and will create a new people from discouraged exiles. The only thing the exiles must do is call upon God. The only thing they must do is believe in God's saving power.

In the Gospel of Mark the events of the first chapter have convinced people that Jesus is able to heal bodily illness. The friends of the paralytic bring him to Jesus in hopes that he will be healed. But Mark continues to heighten the description of Jesus' power over evil, of his amazing authority. Jesus does not do what the man and his friends expect. Rather, he says simply to the paralyzed man, "Your sins are forgiven." There is no description of the reaction of the paralytic, but the scribes present, who have already begun to perceive Jesus as a threat, respond with indignation. No one has power to forgive sins but God. Jesus knows their thoughts and makes clear the meaning of his miracles. The power of Satan has been broken. The power of all evil, not only physical suffering but also sin, will be destroyed with the arrival of the kingdom of God. Even the power of death will be broken, but they cannot understand that yet. Only gradually will they recognize what it means that the power of evil is broken. Only gradually do **we** realize what it means.

In most miracle stories there is a mention of faith. Sometimes the person in need of healing has faith. Sometimes the result of the miracle is an increase of faith. In today's story it is the friends of the sick person who have faith, and that seems to be enough for Jesus to work the miracle. There is an encouraging message in that for us: Our faith may help to heal those we love.

The second reading begins a series of readings from Paul's Second Letter to the Corinthians which will run from the Seventh to the Fourteenth Sunday of Ordinary Time. Paul is concerned that the Corinthians understand the fidelity of God and of Christ. God keeps promises. The ultimate fulfillment of God's promises is in Christ. Christ is "Yes. Amen. Let it be so." In Christ, new life, new creation, comes to all people. In Christ, the kingdom of God arrives.

Irene Nowell, OSB

Questions for Discussion

1. Why do people find it so difficult to believe and understand the power of God's healing love in our lives? Why does our healing depend upon faith?

2. What does it mean to say the power of evil is broken? What difference can it make in our personal lives? What difference can it make in our community?

3. Are there ways we can block God's healing from working in our lives?

For Journaling

1. I continue the healing ministry of Jesus when . . .

2. God wants to heal me by . . .

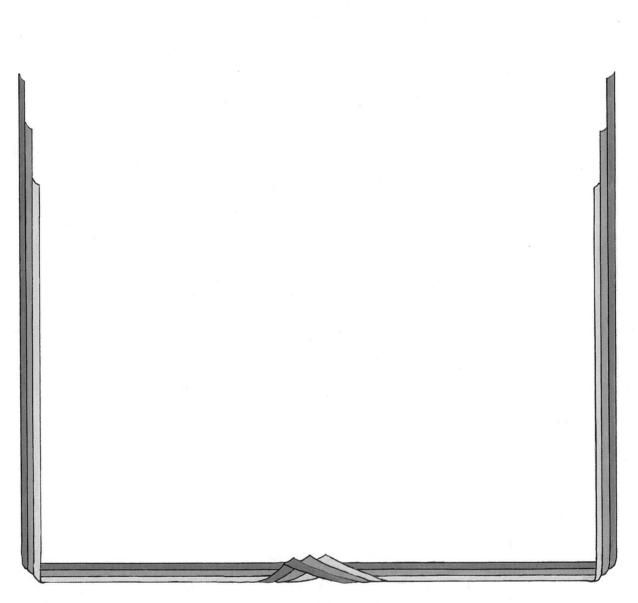

Our Relationship of Love with God

Readings: **Hosea 2:16-17, 21-22 ; 2 Corinthians 3:1-6; Mark 2:18-22**

There are some human relationships which enter the very fiber of our being. Two of the most vital are the relationship between husband and wife and the relationship between father and son. These two relationships were Israel's favorite way to describe the covenant bond between God and the people.

The eighth century B.C.E. prophet Hosea used his own troubled marriage as a model for God's relationship with Israel. Just as his wife had turned from him to other lovers, so Israel had turned from Yahweh to other gods. This turning to other gods, then, this idolatry, is described as adultery, infidelity to her legal husband. What is demanded of Israel is love and fidelity. What God must give Israel in return is love and fidelity.

Chapter two of Hosea begins with divorce proceedings. Yahweh is divorcing Israel and is repudiating claim to her children. Not only has she turned to other lovers (= gods); she has mistakenly believed that Yahweh's gifts of grain, wine, and oil were given her by her lovers. She has used Yahweh's gifts to worship these other gods. Yahweh's heart, however, is not in this divorce. He cannot give her up, no matter what she has done. Therefore He decides to take everything away from her so that she will return to Him. Finally, He will even take the land from her and lead her back into the desert, the desert of exile. Perhaps then she will remember their courtship and covenant-making in the Sinai desert after the exodus from Egypt. Perhaps then the marriage bond can be renewed.

Today's reading is only a portion of the renewal of the marriage between Yahweh and Israel. This bond will last forever. It will be characterized with the qualities of love and fidelity, truth and justice. Israel will again know (= experience) the faithful love of her covenant God.

The marriage symbol of the covenant continues in the New Testament. In today's gospel, Jesus uses the image in a controversy with some Pharisees. He is the groom, the covenant partner in the new covenant. The Church is his bride, bonded to him in love and fidelity.

The point of the argument with these particular Pharisees has precisely to do with the demands of the covenant bond. The Pharisees, in a genuine attempt to be devout, faithful Jews, have developed a whole system of customs and practices—prayers to be said, good works to be done, sacrifices to be made. But in some instances the practices of devotion have become more important than the relationship with God. The Pharisees involved in this argument with Jesus are much more concerned with the custom of fasting than whether Jesus' disciples have a loving, faithful relationship with God. Jesus' response turns them back to the importance of the relationship. Then he continues by implying that they have lost their flexibility and thus lost their capability of accepting surprises in their relationship with God. They are like old wineskins, hardened in the customs and expectations of the past. But any true relationship grows and is full of surprises. Only new wineskins, kept flexible by love and fidelity, can accept the surprises of life with God.

Human relationships are that way, too. We can cease to expect anything from another except the everyday occurrences. We can become rigid in our own living habits and fail to welcome the surprises of a growing relationship. Just as human relationships demand new life every day, so does the covenant relationship with God.

The reading from 2 Corinthians states the same truth in different words. The written, rigid law kills; the Spirit, free, gives life.

Irene Nowell, OSB

29

Questions for Discussion

1. In what ways is our relationship with God like the relationship between a husband and a wife? How is it different? What qualities are suggested in today's readings?

2. When has your relationship with your spouse, friend, or family member demanded flexibility? What surprises mark this relationship?

3. What are some ways you can nourish your relationship with God every day?

For Journaling

1. God has surprised me by . . .

2. What delights me is . . .

Sundays Are Special

Readings: **Deuteronomy 5:12-15; 2 Corinthians 4:6-11; Mark 2:23-3:6**

The Sabbath is one of the most important observances for Israel. It is one of the Ten Commandments (Exodus 20:8-11; Deuteronomy 5:12-15). Breaking of the Sabbath is punishable by death (cf. Exodus 31:14-15). It is the sign of the Sinai covenant between God and the people (Ezekiel 20:12). Keeping it is a way for Israel to be like God, who rested after creation, who gave Israel rest from their slavery. Thus its justification is based on the central events of creation and exodus.

During the Babylonian exile the practices which could be kept anywhere, e.g., circumcision, dietary laws, reading of Scripture, and observing the Sabbath, became major ways for the Jews to retain their identity and to show their fidelity to God. After they returned from exile, there was great concern to remain faithful to the Law so that they would not end up in exile again. Somewhere around the second century B.C.E., a pious group called the Pharisees formed. They began to develop customs to insure that they would never even come close to breaking the Law. They wanted to build "a fence around the Law" to protect it. Their customs were passed on by word of mouth for some centuries, until finally they were collected about A.D. 200. Now they are called the *Talmud.*

Many of these customs had to do with the all-important observance of the Sabbath. Since work was forbidden, some Pharisees set out to define work—so many stitches, so many steps, so heavy a burden, so many strokes of the pen. All activities which began to approach work were forbidden. The disciples in Mark's Gospel are caught in just such a situation. Harvesting is work; picking grain and rubbing it out of the husk is harvesting. Thus the disciples are working on the Sabbath.

Jesus reminds the Pharisees questioning him of the original purpose of the Law. God had released them from the work of slavery in Egypt. Now they were free. A sign of that freedom was the privilege of resting on the Sabbath. God had rested from the work of creation on the seventh day. Human beings, to whom God had entrusted creation, should follow God's example and rest on the seventh day. Some Pharisees had forgotten that the covenant relationship was more important than the covenant Law. Being free to devote attention to God was the purpose of the Sabbath. The Sabbath was designed for the sake of persons, not persons for the Sabbath. To work on the Sabbath is a failure of trust that God cares for creation and is an act of pride. To keep the Sabbath law perfectly, simply for the sake of keeping the law, is also an act of pride. These particular Pharisees had forgotten this.

Just as the miracles are signs of the breaking of Satan's power, the Sabbath is a sign of the kingdom of God which will be an eternal Sabbath. The Pharisees began in the right direction with their intent to keep the Law. Somewhere, however, some of them lost the purpose of the Law. Just as the miracles led them to plot against Jesus, so too Jesus' freedom to interpret the Sabbath led some Pharisees to plot against him. The amazing good news of new life in Jesus leads some people to faith and others to refusal.

In 2 Corinthians Paul describes the paradox of carrying the new life of Jesus in mortal bodies too frail to bear it, and the paradox of carrying the death of Jesus in bodies destined for eternal life. It is the same paradox.

The Sabbath is one way to witness in our ordinary daily lives that we do not live for this moment only. We have a promise of life forever in God's kingdom. Once a week the life of that kingdom breaks into our world and we celebrate the Sabbath.

Irene Nowell, OSB

Questions for Discussion

1. What is the meaning of the Sabbath, of Sunday, for you? How do you observe Sunday?

2. How is it possible to observe the Sabbath, or Sunday, when making a living requires one to work on Sunday?

3. Are there times when we use laws to judge people rather than to free them? How can the Sabbath or Sunday observance free people?

For Journaling

1. On Sunday I like to . . .

2. I observe the Sabbath by . . .

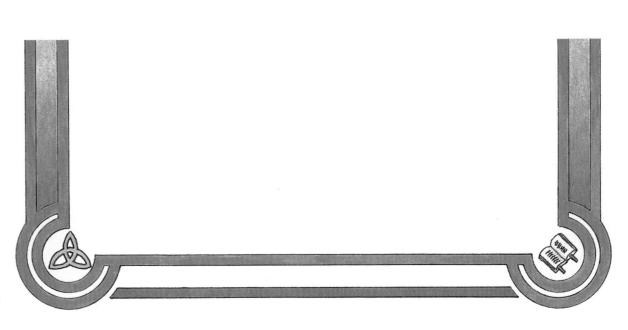

A New Beginning

Readings: **Genesis 9:8-15; 1 Peter 3:18-22; Mark 1:12-15**

The First Sunday of Lent begins the final period of preparation for the catechumens/elect, those who will be baptized at the Easter Vigil. So, during Lent, the whole Church ponders the meaning of baptism with the elect. Today's readings begin that reflection through the images of the flood and the baptism of Jesus. Most of us at some time in our lives have experienced some kind of tragedy, or at least what seemed like tragedy at the time. We lose a loved one, a family or friendship breaks up, we suffer illness, accident, violence, or financial loss. At such times we are overwhelmed by pain and grief. For a time all seems hopeless. But, as we move through the grieving process, we gradually begin to look for hope and new life.

In today's liturgy, we reflect on the tragedy that came upon God's good creation because of human sin. Human beings chose to seek their own selfish interests rather than to care for each other and the rest of creation as God intended. The stories in the first eleven chapters of Genesis illustrate that the result of that choice has been tragedy in families, in communities and nations, in the very earth itself. Yet despite the tragedy, there is hope that the original harmony of creation can be restored.

The first reading is the conclusion of the Noah story. Once the flood which has destroyed the world has subsided, God makes a covenant with Noah and, through Noah, with all creation. God promises that never again will the world be destroyed by water.

This section comes from the Priestly strand of the Pentateuch (the first five books of the Bible.) This Priestly strand was the last to be woven into the story, woven in about the sixth century B.C.E. The creation story in Genesis 1 and the genealogies are also part of this tradition. This section was originally written during the period of the Babylonian exile, when all seemed lost. Thus there is a major concern to reassure the people that they do have a future, that God is faithful to the covenant.

The sign of God's covenant with Noah is the rainbow. The sign is to remind God of His promise. Signs in the other covenants—circumcision in the covenant with Abraham and his descendants, Sabbath in the covenant on Sinai—are to remind the human partners of the covenant.

God's covenant with Noah establishes, in effect, a new creation. The waters of primeval chaos will never again overwhelm the world. All creation, birds and beasts, are renewed in this new creation. For the Priestly author's audience, whose world had seemed destroyed through exile, the story of God's covenant with Noah established new hope.

The First Letter of Peter uses the imagery of the flood and the covenant with Noah as a symbol of baptism. This letter was written to encourage Christians in the face of persecution. A major portion of the letter is devoted to instruction on baptism and Eucharist. The section read today presents Christ's death and resurrection as the true reason for deliverance from sin and death. Through baptism we can be included in that deliverance. Just as eight people were saved through the flood-water of destruction in Noah's time, so Christians are saved by baptism into Christ's death. Just as God's covenant with Noah established a new creation, so too baptism establishes a new creation in Christ. Just as the Noah story encouraged exiled Jews to hope, so the story of Christ's death and resurrection confirms the hope of persecuted Christians.

The gospel story is Mark's very brief presentation of Jesus' baptism, temptation, and early preaching. The Gospel of Mark, the shortest Gospel, is in a hurry to get to the main event of Jesus' death and resurrection. There is a breathless urgency, especially in the first chapters. In these early chapters, as stated previously, *immediately (euthys)* is Mark's favorite word, used eleven times in chapter 1. The sense of urgency helps the reader realize that the time for repentance, for turning life around, is now. Jesus says, "The time of fulfillment has come! The reign of God is at hand. But this is good news! Repent and believe!"

33

The story of Jesus' temptation is told on the First Sunday of Lent every year. The Gospel of Mark says that after Jesus' baptism, the Spirit who had descended upon him drove him into the desert to be tempted by Satan. Those preparing for baptism must know that baptism is not the end of trial and conflict, but baptism into Christ's death. Jesus' example provides them with courage. God remains faithful to the covenant people.

Irene Nowell, OSB

Questions for Discussion

1. Lent is a time for new beginnings. Where is a new beginning needed in your life? In the life of your parish?

2. When you were a child, how did you observe Lent? What has been the most significant Lent for you?

3. What will you do to strengthen your covenant relationship with God this Lent?

For Journaling

Jesus goes to the desert to be tempted by Satan. What temptation in your life keeps you from living your life with joy and peace?

Or:

1. When I see a rainbow, I feel . . .

2. The rainbow is a sign of God's faithfulness. I have experienced God's faithfulness when . . .

The Cost of Discipleship

Readings: Genesis 22:1-2, 9, 10-13, 15-18; Romans 8:31-34; Mark 9:2-10

In Cycle B, the first reading for each of the Sundays of Lent picks up a covenant theme. A covenant is a solemn agreement which binds two or more parties. Every day we enter into agreements, contracts, or covenants which bind us to some obligation. Some are formal, with the expectations on both parties clearly set forth in a legally binding contract, signed and notarized by official witnesses. Others are more informal, but demanding in another sense, e.g., giving one's word. Others, such as marriage, require a total giving of self on the part of each partner. Baptism is this latter kind of covenant, a covenant with God.

On the Second Sunday of Lent, the story of Abraham's testing is told. God had promised Abraham land, descendants, and a special relationship with God. Initially Abraham has only promises, but, in spite of his old age, Isaac is born, living hope of God's fidelity. But God tests Abraham's faith by asking of him the sacrifice of the only tangible sign of the covenant that he has, his son. The test is a terrible demand. Does Abraham love God more than God's promises? Does Abraham trust God?

Abraham's characteristic response throughout the story is, "Here I am" (22:1, 11). He makes no objection to God. He acts in simple unquestioning obedience. This obedience, according to God's messenger, is the reason that Abraham will receive the covenant promises. Because of his obedience, he will be blessed and all nations of the earth blessed in him (cf. Genesis 12:2-3). Thus the sin of disobedience (Genesis 3:6) which brought alienation and death is healed at least in promise by obedience. Abraham's obedience will bring blessing and life.

Abraham lived among the Canaanites, who worshiped the god Moloch. The background for this story is the Canaanite practice of sacrificing the firstborn son to Moloch. The Canaanites believed the firstborn belonged to the god. They sacrificed the firstborn son to the god to guarantee the birth of many sons. This idea is reflected in two ways in the Old Testament. In Exodus 13, instructions are given for redeeming the firstborn son, who belongs to Yahweh. But never is the firstborn to be sacrificed. And the practice is forbidden and is condemned (cf. 1 Kings 16:34; 2 Kings 3:27). Abraham's story emphasizes the fact that God demands obedience, not sacrifice (cf. 1 Samuel 15:21-23).

The reading from Romans presents a New Testament parallel to God's demand on Abraham. God does not actually demand the sacrifice of Abraham's son as a price of the covenant relationship. On the other hand, God sacrifices the life of His own Son to preserve the covenant relationship with humankind.

Today's reading is toward the conclusion of Paul's impassioned testimony that there is no condemnation for those who are in Christ Jesus (cf. Romans 8:1). Only God or Christ could condemn, but it is through them that salvation comes. Therefore, nothing can separate us from the love of God in Christ Jesus.

On the Second Sunday of Lent every year, the gospel reading is the story of Jesus' transfiguration. The other two readings have centered on the relationship between "Father" and "Son." The transfiguration is a physical illustration of the relationship between Jesus and his Father. The voice that comes from the cloud proclaims him the beloved son. His appearance is that of a person completely transparent to the presence and will of God.

The transfiguration is a manifestation of God full of symbolism. The images of cloud and mountain suggest God's appearance at the covenant-making on Mount Sinai (cf. Exodus 19). Moses, major figure in the exodus and the Sinai covenant, represents the Law. Elijah, great ninth-century prophet of Israel, represents the prophets. Thus the two major periods of Israel's history and the two major divisions of Israel's Scripture are represented in these two figures.

Jesus' appearance is an anticipation of his resurrection glory, a vision of the human completely penetrated by God. The three favorite disciples—Peter, James, and John—are forbidden to tell the vision until the resurrection, lest they miss the point that the Messiah could not come to glory without suffering, a major theological assertion of the Gospel of Mark.

Irene Nowell, OSB

Questions for Discussion

1. What are covenants you have made in your life? Which have demanded the most of you? Why do you make that sacrifice?

2. The transfiguration is a manifestation of God. Can you name a moment in your life when you felt God was especially present to you? What effect did that experience have on your life?

For Journaling

1. The covenant that has changed my life the most is . . .

2. To give oneself totally means . . .

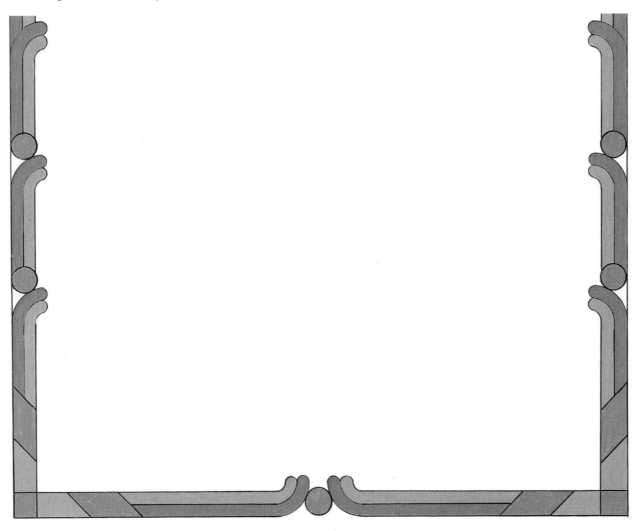

Christ Jesus, hear our humble petitions,
for we have sinned against you.
Glory to the Father, and to the Son, and to the
Holy Spirit
Listen to us, O Lord, and have mercy, for we
have sinned against you.

:le of Mary
hon Whoever drinks the water that I shall give will
      never be thirsty again, says the Lord.

and Praise #123 MY SOUL REJOICES

phon (Repeat as above) Whoever drinks the water...

rcessions

onse: Lord, be gracious to your people.

FATHER

YER AND DISMISSAL

Turn away from sin

and be faithful

to the GOSPEL

EVENING PRAYER

Leader: God, come to my assistance.

   All: Lord, make haste to help me.

Leader: Glory to the Father, and to the Son,
         and to the Holy Spirit.

   All: As it was in the beginning, is now,
         and will be forever. Amen.

   HYMN

Antiphon 1 Lord, all powerful King, free us for the sake
            of your name. Give us time to turn from our
            sins.

Psalm 110:1-5, 7 The Messiah, king and priest

The Lord's revelation to my Master:
"Sit on my right:
your foes I will put beneath your feet."

The Lord will yield from Zion
your scepter of power:
rule in the midst of all your foes.

A prince from the day of your birth
on the holy mountains;
from the womb before the dawn I begot you.

The Lord has sworn an oath he will not change.
"You are a priest for ever,
a priest like Melchizedek of old."

The Master standing at your right hand
will shatter kings in the day of his great wrath.

He shall drink from the stream by the wayside
and therefore he shall lift up his head.

Glory to the Father, and to the Son, and to the
Holy Spirit.

As it was in the beginning, is now,
and will be forever. Amen.

Antiphon   Lord, all powerful King, free us for the sake
           of your name. Give us time to turn from our sins.

PSALM PRAYER

Antiphon 2 We have been redeemed by the precious blood of
            Christ, the lamb without blemish.

Psalm 111   God's marvelous works

I will thank the Lord with all my heart
in the meeting of the just and their assembly.
Great are the works of the Lord;
to be pondered by all who love them.

Majestic and glorious his work,
his justice stands firm for ever.
He makes us remember his wonders.
The Lord is compassion and love.

He gives food to those who fear him;
keeps his covenant ever in mind.
He has shown his might to his people
by giving them the lands of the nations.

His works are justice and truth:
his precepts are all of them sure,
standing firm for ever and ever:
they are made in uprightness and truth.

He has sent deliverance to his people
and established his covenant for ever.
Holy his name, to be feared.

To fear the Lord is the first stage of wisdom;
all who do so prove themselves wise.
His praise shall last for ever!

Glory to the Father, and to the Son, and to the
Holy Spirit.

As it was in the beginning, is now,
and will be forever. Amen.

Antiphon We have been redeemed by the p.
          Christ, the lamb without blemis

PSALM PRAYER

Antiphon 3 Ours were the sufferings he bo
            ours the torments he endured.

Canticle 1 Peter 2:21-24 Christ accepts h

Christ suffered for you,
and left you an example
to have you follow in his footsteps.

He did no wrong; no deceit was found in his m
When he was insulted, he returned no insult.

When he was made to suffer, he did not counter
Instead he delivered himself up to the One who

In his own body he brought your sins to the cro
so that all of us, dead to sin, could live in ac
with God's will. By his wounds you were healed.

Glory to the Father, and to the Son, and to the
Holy Spirit.

As it was in the beginning, is now,
and will be forever. Amen.

Antiphon Ours were the sufferings he bore;
          ours the torments he endured.

READING

RESPONSE:
LEADER: Listen to us, O Lord, and have mercy, for we
         have sinned against you.
   ALL: Listen to us, O Lord, and have mercy, for we
         have sinned against you.

LEADER
ALL
LEADER

ALL

Canti
Antip

Glory

Anti

Inte

Resp

OUR

PRA

The Covenant

Readings: Exodus 20:1–17; 1 Corinthians 1:22–25; John 2:13–25

Families, organizations, communities, nations—all have rules, some formal, others informal. These rules allow a number of people to work together in peace to achieve the goals of the group. Rules help to define the rights of the individuals in the group and allow for the freedom of all. Responsible membership in these groups requires that we abide by the group's rules.

Again this Sunday, the first reading draws from the theme of covenant. In every covenant, every binding relationship, there are duties and responsibilities. Every covenant implies law. The central law of the covenant made on Mount Sinai is expressed in what we call the Ten Commandments or the Decalogue. These Ten Commandments, with some variations, are repeated twice: once in Exodus when the Sinai story is told and again in Deuteronomy 5 when the story is repeated.

The form in which the law of the Ten Commandments is expressed is absolute. The command is stated simply with no conditions: Do this; don't do that. This form is almost unique to Israel. Usually her neighbors expressed their law as case law: In such a situation, do this. Israel also used case law (cf. Exodus 22:1–17), but the central statement is absolute law. Some commandments have reasons given, such as the first and third commandments. The fourth commandment, honor your father and mother, has a reward: long life.

The Ten Commandments are the central expression of covenanted life with Israel's God. They outline the characteristic relationships with God and with neighbor. Stated positively, the primary demands of the covenant are love and fidelity (cf. Deuteronomy 6:4–9; Leviticus 19:1–18).

The reading from 1 Corinthians is part of Paul's defense of his preaching in Corinth. He claims it is not wisdom and eloquence which makes his preaching powerful, but rather it is the power of Christ crucified. This latter power seems to satisfy no one.

As Paul puts it, Jews demand "signs." Signs are an important part of Israel's theology. The plagues in Egypt which forced the pharaoh to release the people are usually called "signs and wonders" (Psalms 78:43, 105:27). Covenants are often marked by signs: the rainbow for the covenant with Noah (Genesis 9:12); circumcision for the covenant with Abraham (Genesis 17:11); the Sabbath for the Sinai covenant (Ezekiel 20:20). Signs, however, are only useful for the message they convey; they can never be sought simply for their own sake. In Israel's life, signs always convey the message of the presence and power of God. Only those who are willing to hear the message should seek signs. For those who can see, Christ is the ultimate sign of the presence and power of God.

Greeks look for "wisdom." The central premise of wisdom is the knowledge of how to live well. This knowledge about living comes from the experience of living; it is not received through revelation. The many expressions of Greek philosophy search for the meaning of life in order to be able to live well. Paul proclaims that true life comes through Christ. The knowledge that God has shared in human suffering gives an entirely new answer to the absurdity of suffering. The knowledge that Christ leads us to a risen life gives an entirely new answer to the absurdity of death. God's folly is wiser than our wisdom; God's weakness is more powerful than our strength.

There is a subtle link between the second reading and the gospel. The temple is revered in Israel as a sign of the presence of God. Jesus cleanses the sign because it is no longer conveying the message. He also adds a further message: "Destroy this temple and in three days I will raise it up." He transfers the sign of God's presence from the temple to his own body, risen from death.

The telling of the story of the cleansing of the temple is much earlier in the Gospel of John than it is in the synoptic Gospels, Matthew, Mark, and Luke. In all the Gospels, however, it is a premonition of the passion. Jesus will be accused in the trial of having committed blasphemy by talking about destruction of the temple, sign of the presence of God (Mark 14:58). The result of that trial will be the condemnation to death of Jesus, sign of the presence of God. The resurrection will be the sign of the presence of God expressed in the new temple of his risen body.

Irene Nowell, OSB

Questions for Discussion

1. What are signs that God is or is not the center of your life? Of our country's life?

2. The temple was a sign to the people of Israel of God's presence. What are signs to you of God's presence?

3. When are the Commandments a sign of the presence of God? Can a devotion to the Law become an empty sign? In what way?

For Journaling

1. I place God in the center of my life when I . . .

2. Write a letter to your children or grandchildren telling them how to be happy. In what ways does your letter reflect the wisdom of the Commandments?

Grace

Readings: **2 Chronicles 36:14-16, 19-23; Ephesians 2:4-10; John 3:14-21**

For each of us there are moments when we are suddenly aware of the goodness of life, of the way we have been gifted. We wonder how we could have been so lucky, what we could have done to deserve all this. Often it happens as we catch a glimpse of a loved one, a child, or an elderly parent. Or we see a sunset, a field of grain waving in the wind, or admire our own handiwork. It may happen as we sit for a moment in the evening or lie in bed in the early morning listening to the singing of the birds. It may happen in the busyness of our daily work, or in a gathering at the parish church for a family or parish celebration. These moments themselves are gifts, helping us to recognize all of life as a gift. They move us to raise our hearts in gratitude to God. Our loved ones, the beauty of nature, the parish church, which have been occasions for such revelations, become signs for us of God's presence in our lives.

The temple was such a sign for the people of Israel. The image of the temple, prominent in last Sunday's gospel, reappears in the first reading for this Sunday. The selection is from the final chapter of 2 Chronicles. Chronicles was written after the Babylonian exile as a reinterpretation of history for the new situation in which the people found themselves. A major focus of hope for the returned community was the rebuilt temple, a sign of the return of God's presence. The destruction of the former temple was seen as a punishment for their sins and a fulfillment of the prophets' warnings.

In 587 B.C.E., the Babylonians had destroyed Jerusalem and taken many of its inhabitants into exile. They remained in Babylon until 539 when Cyrus the Persian came into power. Cyrus's policy toward the religious beliefs of his subjects was one of tolerance, provided the people prayed for him. Thus he decreed that the Jews could return to Jerusalem and rebuild the temple. The return in fact was not as glorious as the people hoped. Restoring the land was difficult, and there was widespread poverty. With the encouragement of the two prophets, Haggai and Zechariah, however, the second temple was finally completed and dedicated in 515, a little over seventy years after its destruction.

The Jews saw both exile and restoration as acts of God. The Letter to the Ephesians emphasizes the fact that God's salvation is a gift, not something earned by human effort. The compassionate God who attempted to save Israel through the prophets, but who finally banished them into exile (cf. 2 Chronicles), tries a new approach. In order to save human beings, who are still dead in sin, God recreates them in Christ Jesus to lead a life of good deeds.

In the Old Testament the major covenant virtues manifested in God and demanded of human beings are love and fidelity. In Ephesians we are told again that it is because of God's great love and abundant mercy that we are brought to life in Christ. Salvation is sheer gift, given by the favor of God. God's only reward for the gift is the manifestation of His goodness, shown through our salvation. From any angle, human beings are the winners.

The gift of God is visible only to the eyes of faith. In today's section from the Gospel of John, Jesus attempts to explain to Nicodemus the truth seen in faith. A statement of the central truth of Christianity is imbedded in this gospel: "God so loved the world that he gave his only Son, that whoever believes in him may not die, but may have eternal life." Jesus has just explained to Nicodemus the difference between human life as we know it and the gift of eternal life. Now he describes the contrast between those who choose eternal life and those who reject it. Those who choose eternal life receive it because of faith in Christ, and their faith is demonstrated in good deeds, which they are happy to bring to the light. Those who reject eternal life reject it because of lack of faith, and their lack of faith is demonstrated in evil deeds which they hide from the light. In any case, judgment results from human choice. The gift of salvation is given; human beings choose it or reject it. Human beings choose or reject life.

Irene Nowell, OSB

Questions for Discussion

1. The temple was a sign to the Israelites of God's presence with them. What are special holy places for you? Why do they carry that meaning for you?

2. Jesus shifts the meaning of the symbol of the temple to talk about his own body. In what way is your body a sign of the presence of God? What destroys this temple? How can it be restored?

For Journaling

Life is God's gift, ours for the choosing.

1. I choose life when I . . .

2. I choose death when I . . .

3. God's gift is . . .

Paschal Mystery

Readings: Jeremiah 31:31-34; Hebrews 5:7-9; John 12:20-33

On this last Sunday of Lent before Passion Week, we ponder the mystery of life and death, of life that overcomes death. All around us the new life of springtime is overcoming the death of winter. We bury seeds, small packages of life, in the soil. The seed is transformed so that the seed is no more, but in its place, new life grows in the form of a plant. The seed that is planted has within it the genetic code that determines what the new plant will be. The new life that is within the seed needs only the right conditions in order to spring into life. In today's readings we reflect on new life and new beginnings.

The covenant theme which we have pondered throughout Lent comes to a climax today with Jeremiah's description of Yahweh's new covenant. This short passage consists of a description of the state of the old covenant and the promise of a new covenant. The old covenant, which was made at Sinai after God had delivered the people from Egypt, was a conditional covenant. It was dependent both on the fidelity of God and on the fidelity of the people. God had remained faithful, but the people had not. Thus the covenant was broken and God had to re-establish order, literally to ''lord'' it over the people.

But the new covenant is to be radically different from the old. It is true that in some ways it is the same. In both covenants there is a demand of love and fidelity. There will continue to be law. The relationship between God and the people is expressed in the same covenant formula: I will be your God and you will be my people. But the radical difference is found in the location of the covenant document. The old covenant was written in stone; the new covenant will be written on the people's hearts. The old covenant had to be learned; in the new covenant all will know, that is, experience the Lord and the covenant Law. With the new covenant the old sins are forgotten by God, and whatever is not remembered by God does not exist. The new covenant is a new beginning.

Both New Testament readings continue the description of the mystery of our redemption in Christ. On this Sunday before Holy Week, the reading from the Letter to the Hebrews points out the price of our salvation. Jesus prayed to God who was able to save him from death. The synoptic Gospels, (Matthew, Mark, and Luke), give a somewhat longer description of this prayer in their description of Jesus in Gethsemane the night before he died (see Mark 14:32-42). The first movement of the prayer is a plea to be saved from death. But the second movement is an acceptance of the will of the Father. ''He learned obedience from what he suffered.'' It is this double movement of the prayer which makes Jesus perfect and makes him the source of salvation for all who in turn obey him. Sin and suffering come through disobedience. Salvation comes through obedience bought at the price of suffering. Jesus' prayer was heard: through death he was saved from death; through his death all were given life.

The passage from the Gospel of John treats the same mystery with different imagery. Two key words of the passage are *hour* and *glorify*. The ''hour'' is at once the moment of Jesus' death, resurrection, and exaltation. Jesus prays to be saved from that hour, yet it is the hour of his glorification also. It is the hour which sets the purpose for his life. He prays for the glory of the Father. In turn, that obedience is what glorifies Jesus.

The paradox of life in the midst of death is stated several ways. The image of the grain of wheat which dies to produce life sets the stage. The paradox is stated directly: The one who loves life loses it; the one who sacrifices life gains eternal life. Jesus is the primary example. Finally, the play on the words *lifted up* unites the apparent opposites of humiliating death and regal exaltation. Jesus will be lifted up on the cross to die in a humiliating and agonizing form of execution. In that same moment Jesus will be exalted as the glorious king who draws all to himself and thus to eternal life.

41

All of us approach the suffering in our lives with reluctance, even dread and fear. Yet, as we look back over our lives, we can often point to the "new life" that came about because of that suffering. We too learn to listen to God through what we suffer. In that listening, in that obedience, and in the power and grace bestowed on us by Jesus' once-for-all victorious sacrifice, we too find eternal life.

Irene Nowell, OSB

Questions for Discussion

1. During this past year, where have you seen the paradox of life in the midst of death?

2. As we mature, we begin to internalize the rules and customs which our parents and teachers taught us. Can you recall the struggle to accept those rules when you were younger? When did they become a valued part of you?

3. What does it mean to have the law of God written in your heart?

For Journaling

1. When I face suffering . . .

2. When I think about all the suffering in the world today . . .

3. Suffering brings new life when . . .

Holy Week

Readings: **Mark 11:1-10; Isaiah 50:4-7; Philippians 2:6-11; Mark 14:1-15:47**

We are coming to the end of Lent and to the most important celebration of the liturgical year. On Thursday Lent will end; the Easter Triduum will begin with the celebration of the Lord's Supper and culminate in the Easter Vigil celebrated in the dark before Easter Sunday morning. These three days, (*Triduum* means "three days"), bring together in one celebration the whole meaning of life for us as Christians. Although our culture may make Christmas a bigger celebration than Easter, there would be no Christmas celebration if Jesus had not died and been raised from the dead.

On Passion Sunday, better known as Palm Sunday, we remember the triumphant entry of Jesus into Jerusalem. This was the first event of that momentous week which culminated in his death and resurrection. We too form a procession and wave palms to open our celebration of the great Christian Passover. Our procession is an act of faith in the whole paschal mystery, for we know how the story we tell this week is going to turn out.

As we stand with the blessed palm branches in our hands, we listen to the story of that first Palm Sunday. Jesus had come to Jerusalem for the celebration of the Jewish Passover. It was a week-long celebration in which they recalled and reclaimed their liberation from slavery in Egypt. It was a time to retell the story to the next generation, so that they would understand what it meant to belong to this chosen people. Many of the pilgrims had heard Jesus speak and had seen the signs and wonders that accompanied his preaching. Others had heard about him. Many had begun to believe that Jesus might be the messiah. The feast of the Passover would be a fitting time to claim his role as messiah.

But the understanding of messiah which most of these people held was different from Jesus' understanding. On this occasion, Jesus used an image from the Book of the prophet Zechariah. Instead of mounting on a horse, the mount of generals and conquerors, Jesus rides a donkey, as peaceful people did. Many of the Jews of his time expected the messiah to come with great power to conquer their enemies and re-establish the kingdom of Israel. In this image Jesus shows that the real path to salvation is the way of pardon and nonviolence. Many of the Jews could not recognize such a messiah. Some of those who hoped for a triumphant political announcement from Jesus during this festival ended up in the crowd who denied him later that week.

After the procession, the mood of the liturgy changes, and we begin to ponder the events that followed that glorious entrance into Jerusalem. The first reading from Isaiah 50 is taken from the third "Song of the Suffering Servant." It shows us the faithful disciple whose faithfulness is founded on the fidelity of God. The passage was originally written about someone else, possibly about a prophet or about the people as a whole, or both. However, when we read this passage, we immediately think about Jesus. The servant is also an image of the Christian who recognizes that, even in the midst of the sufferings of life, God is with him or her.

The second reading, taken from Paul's letter to the Philippians, is a quotation from an early Christian hymn that is sort of a creed. This hymn proclaims the meaning of Jesus' death and resurrection. Even though Jesus was God, he obediently accepted the humiliation of the cross, and God raised him in glory. As we read the passion story from the Gospel according to Mark, we keep these images in mind.

The stories of the passion were probably the first part of the Gospels to be written down. There are more details here than in any other part of the Gospel. In Mark's Gospel, we see the powers of evil reaching a high point in this story. Yet Mark would have us know that the power of God has rendered the evil powerless.

The story of the passion is not just about an historical event. It has another dimension, for it calls us to see how that story is being re-enacted in our own lives personally and as a people. We have seen the power of evil in ourselves and in our world. We see the evil of selfishness, the loss of personal integrity, the loss of a sense of public responsibility, the threat of nuclear or environmental disaster. Sometimes it seems that the evil will triumph and that we are alone in our struggle against it. We retell the story to remember that God is with us in our struggle. We remember and are strengthened by the knowledge that Jesus has fundamentally triumphed over evil, sin, and death. Yet God's way is not some magic trick to release us from the evil. In the power of Christ, God is with us in the suffering and in the dying of our everyday lives, and not just at the end of our life on earth. We can expect that, through these sufferings and deaths, we can be freed from evil and grow into a new life.

Holy Thursday Readings: Exodus 12:1-8, 11-14; 1 Corinthians 11:23-26; John 13:1-15

Lent officially ends and the Triduum begins with the celebration of the Lord's Supper on Holy Thursday evening. We gather as Jesus and his disciples gathered in the evening. In the first reading, we read the instructions given to the Jewish people for the celebration of the Passover. It was such a celebration for which Jesus and his disciples gathered that evening. They ate the lamb that had been sacrificed and remembered how the blood of the lamb on the doorpost had saved their ancestors from death. They remembered how they had eaten their bread in haste before they set out on the road toward freedom.

When we Christians read these instructions, we think of our Jewish brothers and sisters who still meet on the Passover to eat this meal and to recall who they are as God's chosen people. But we also think of Jesus whose blood has saved us from sin and death. We remember that on this night Jesus ended the Passover meal by giving us the sacrament of his body and blood.

The second reading, taken from Paul's letter to the Corinthians, is the earliest Christian written text we have which describes the Eucharist in the early Church. At the Last Supper, Jesus offered a new meaning for the bread and wine of the Passover meal. Aware of what awaited him the next day, Jesus gave them the bread and wine. "This is my body," he said. "This cup is the new covenant in my blood," he said. Here in powerful sign, Jesus showed them the meaning of his death and resurrection. He was pouring himself out in love for the sake of the Father and for his brothers and sisters. Then he told them to continue to do this in memory of him. Every time we eat this bread and wine, which has become the body and blood of Christ, we are present again at that total giving of himself for us.

The gospel reading is taken from John's Gospel. This is the only story we have about the Last Supper in John's Gospel. Here again, Jesus shows in sign the meaning of his death and resurrection. Jesus takes the role of a slave, washing the dusty feet of the disciples. And he also gives a command. We too are to wash one another's feet.

Following the homily at this celebration, the pastor washes the feet of twelve members of the congregation, a gesture recalling Jesus' action. This ritual is a sign for us of our ministry in the Church. Each of us is called to serve others as Jesus did. And, like the apostles, we too must accept the ministry of others, for it is Jesus who ministers to us in them. This is what it means to be a disciple. This is what it means to celebrate Eucharist. We too must love and serve one another with great reverence.

These readings help to set the tone for the Triduum. They tell us the meaning of what we remember and celebrate. This is not an historical re-enactment as you might find at some national historical site. Rather, the paschal mystery is about our lives today, as well as about Jesus' death and resurrection so many years ago. Jesus shows us that suffering and death, when accepted out of love for God and others, can lead to new life. His suffering and death offer new life to us even in the middle of our own suffering and death.

At the end of tonight's service, the altar is stripped. The signs of celebration are all gone as we remember Jesus' long night of suffering in prison. We are invited to stop and spend some time in prayer before the Blessed Sacrament, remembering the love with which Jesus gave himself.

Good Friday Readings: Isaiah 52:13-53:12; Hebrews 4:14-16, 5:7-9; John 18:1-19:42

Today we celebrate the Lord's passion and death. It is a solemn and serious celebration, but it is not simply a sad event that we are recalling. We know that Jesus has risen from the dead, so our celebration of this event focuses on its whole meaning. This is a day of fast, but not a fast of mourning. It is a fast of anticipation, fasting from food and work and entertainment, the distractions of our everyday lives, in order to focus on this great event. We gather to celebrate the Lord's passion, to express the meaning of this event for us as Christians.

The core of the celebration is the reading of the Scriptures, especially the story of the passion. We begin with a reading from Isaiah 52, the fourth Servant Song. The song portrays one who suffers for the sake of the people, and Christian tradition uses this image to interpret the suffering and death of Jesus.

A short reading from the Letter to the Hebrews portrays Jesus as the great high priest who offers a perfect sacrifice in his loving obedience to the Father. His obedience restores our relationship with God which had been disrupted by our disobedience. We read the story of the passion as it is told in the Gospel according to John. As John tells the story, he emphasizes the Christian's faith in Jesus' divinity. Jesus has conquered sin and death.

Having pondered Jesus' gift of himself for the salvation of all humankind, we turn our thoughts to all those for whom Christ died. Gathered as Jesus' followers, we pray for the Church, the pope, the clergy, and all the people. We pray for those preparing for baptism and for the unity of the Church. We pray for the Jews, for people who do not believe in Christ, and for those who do not believe in God. We pray for those in public office and for all those in any special need. With Jesus today we hold all people and all things in our hearts.

Following the intercessions, we venerate the cross. The meaning of the cross has changed for us. Christians no longer see the cross as an instrument of shame and death. No, the cross is now a sign of Christ's victory, a symbol of glory. The cross has become a sign that God is with us in Christ in our suffering and our dying, and that God offers us new life in the saving victory of Jesus Christ. Our veneration of the cross is solemn, but the solemnity is touched by our realization of the power of the cross.

The service closes with Holy Communion, using the Eucharistic bread consecrated at yesterday's celebration. After the service, the altar is stripped again. Everything is bare as we remember the burial of Jesus' body in the tomb.

Holy Saturday is a quiet day of anticipation and preparation for the celebration of the Easter Vigil.

Easter Vigil Readings: Genesis 1:1-2:2; Genesis 22:1-18; Exodus 14:15-15:1; Isaiah 54:5-14; Isaiah 55:1-11; Baruch 3:9-15, 32-4:4; Ezekiel 36:16-28; Romans 6:3-11; Mark 16:1-18

The Easter Vigil is the most significant and important celebration in the whole liturgical year. In this celebration we celebrate the meaning of the world, of life and death, as they have been revealed to us in the death and resurrection of Christ. We bring new members into the Church, baptizing them that they may die and rise with Christ. As we baptize these new members, we ponder the meaning of our own baptism and are renewed in our profession of faith.

The Vigil is divided into four parts:

1. The Service of Light, which includes the blessing of the new fire, the blessing of the Easter candle, the sharing of the light, and the Easter proclamation or *Exultet*

2. The Liturgy of the Word which tells the story of our salvation in five to nine readings from the Old and New Testaments

3. The Liturgy of Baptism when new members are reborn in the waters of baptism

4. The Liturgy of the Eucharist when the whole Christian community is brought to the table which the Lord has prepared through his death and resurrection

We gather in the dark, a sign of the darkness of sin and evil, the darkness in our own lives and in the whole world, the darkness that keeps us from seeing clearly who we are and who are those around us. And we light a candle, sign of the true Light who enlightens our darkness. In his light we can begin to see who we are and grow into the community we have been created to be. The rituals of lighting and blessing of the new fire, of the singing of the Easter proclamation, reach back to pre-Christian times and humanity's longing for the Light to enlighten our darkness. We call all of creation to rejoice with us in the Light of Christ which banishes darkness and calls us to new and everlasting life.

The reading of the word of God is the fundamental element of the Easter Vigil. For pastoral reasons, the number of readings may be reduced, but at least three readings from the Old Testament or Hebrew Scriptures should be retained. As we ponder these readings and respond in song and prayer, we ponder the mystery of human life, of our own life and our destiny as children of God. The following reflection on the readings, adapted from an article first written for *Homily Service,* can provide one possible guide to understanding the choice, arrangement, and meaning of those readings.

> *This is the night when Jesus broke the chains of death and rose triumphant from the grave (Exultet). This is the night when Christians everywhere stay awake to remember Christ's resurrection and watch for his coming. Because the watch lasts through the night, there is time to tell salvation's story from the beginning, rehearsing all the high points between creation and resurrection. The interplay of reading and response gives us a key to this night's progression of thought.*
>
> *The story begins with creation. This patterned account presents eight works of creation performed in six days, completed by God's rest on the seventh day. Stereotyped phrases, each repeated seven times, shape the account: "God saw how good it was," "and so it happened." God creates by word—"let there be"— and action—"let us make"—naming the works of creation and blessing them. The final work is the human creature made in God's image, male and female. The psalm (104 or 33) prays that the spirit of God (the mighty wind that hovered over the waters at the beginning) be sent back to renew creation.*

But the human creature, created free, chose to serve self rather than the Creator, and the rest of the story traces the return back to God. We tell the stories of our ancestors in the faith. Abraham, the first to believe, is portrayed at the moment of his greatest test. He obeyed in silence when God called him to leave home and family (Genesis 12:4); he questioned but believed the promise of land and descendants (Genesis 15:2-6). He and Sarah laughed when the promise became specific in "Isaac" ("laughter," Genesis 17:17). Now God demands the child's sacrifice as a sign of the covenant, and again Abraham obeys in silence. God interrupts the sacrifice and provides a substitute, praising Abraham's faith and renewing the blessing that will come to all nations through him, now specifically because of his radical obedience. God, who will sacrifice the beloved son on the cross for the covenant's sake, rewards Abraham and all who follow in faith for the willingness to make such a sacrifice. The psalm (16) could well be put in the mouths of Isaac and Jesus, those two sons offered for the sake of the bond between God and humankind: "Keep me safe, O God, you are my hope."

The central event of Israel's history is the exodus from Egypt. A helpless group of people, whose only strength is God, face Egypt's army. The spirit over the waters of chaos is replaced by the strong east wind, and God's people emerge victorious from the sea. The story combines two accounts, one in which a strong wind dries a swamp enough for people to cross on foot, but not enough for chariots to drive through, and the other in which water stands like a wall beside Israel, but returns to its fluid state to drown the Egyptians. The message in both is the same: "Thus you will know that I am the Lord," the one who will be there for you. The song of Miriam and Moses praises God's mighty work of liberation.

The readings from Isaiah encourage Israel to believe that God, who delivered them from bondage in Egypt, can deliver them now from exile in Babylon. Their creation as a people through the exodus will be paralleled by their re-creation in a new exodus. The broken marriage bond of the covenant will be renewed; the people will be fed and sustained by God as they once were in the desert; the promise to David will be confirmed, that his descendant will always reign over the people; and God's creative word will accomplish all this. Our response is a song of praise for deliverance (Psalm 30) and an echo of our exodus song.

The next readings emphasize different aspects of the renewed covenant. Baruch was written after the exile, and the form in which we have it dates from the first century before Christ. The readings extol the Law, Israel's gift of life from God. To know the Law is to know how to be like God and to find wisdom, through which God created the world. The readings from Ezekiel return to the images of creation and exodus, wind (spirit, breath) and water, the promise of a new exodus, creation, and covenant. Through Israel's regathering, the nations will know that the Lord is God, present for the people. The psalms express our longing for God's presence.

The final two readings are from the New Testament. In the letter to the Romans, Paul reminds us that the way we are inserted in the story—the way we share in creation, exodus, and the return from exile—is through baptism into Christ's death. Thus we are delivered from sin's slavery and created anew in the resurrection. The images of water and wind (spirit) return in the story's culmination. Sin and death are defeated once for all; new life has come through Christ's victory.

The alleluia leads to the news we await throughout this night. "He has been raised up. . . . He is going ahead of you to Galilee, where you will see him just as he told you." The night is over. The day has come.

Based on an essay by Irene Nowell, OSB, which appeared in Homily Service, (20 April 1987). Copyright, The Liturgical Conference, 1017 Twelfth St. NW, Washington, DC 02005. All rights reserved. Used with permission.

Having retold the story of our salvation, we invite the catechumens/elect to enter into the story through baptism. We call on all the saints to pray for us and the elect. We bless water, recalling its meaning throughout our history. With the elect, we profess our faith through our baptismal vows. The elect are baptized, confirmed, and brought to the Eucharistic table.

The Easter Triduum is an event to be experienced. It speaks to us of the very meaning of our lives. But our lives are always changing. Each year as we celebrate the Triduum and reflect on the meaning of life and death, we discover new depths of its mystery. Participating in the Easter Vigil helps us to discover and remember who we are as Christians. If we stay away from the Vigil for too long, we may forget what our lives are all about.

Jeanita Strathman Lapa and Eleanor Suther, OSB

For Reflection and Discussion

1. When I was a child, Holy Week was . . .
2. The Easter Triduum I remember best . . .
3. What I like best about the Easter Triduum . . .
4. I am finding new life . . .

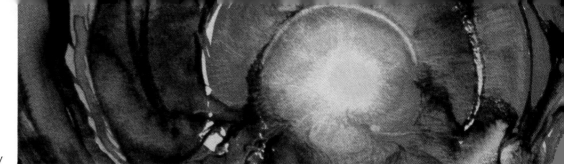

The Lord Is Risen

Readings: Acts 10:34, 37-43; Colossians 3:1-4 or 1 Corinthians 5:6-8; John 20:1-9 or Mark 16:1-8

The Easter Sunday celebration properly begins with the seven Old Testament and two New Testament readings of the Easter Vigil. The Sunday morning readings must be understood in that context.

The first reading for Sunday morning is from the Acts of the Apostles. Acts has traditionally been read during the celebration of the fifty days of Easter. The book is a companion volume to the Gospel of Luke and the story of the early Church's witness to the resurrection.

The reading for this Sunday is a part of Peter's speech on the occasion of the baptism of Cornelius. Speeches make up a significant part of Acts and are a major vehicle for Luke's theology. The scene for this speech is the house of a Gentile, Cornelius, who wishes to be instructed in the new Way of Christianity. Peter, who must be convinced by a vision that a Gentile is not unclean, begins his speech of instruction. Before Peter has finished, however, the Holy Spirit descends upon all present, including the Gentiles! Peter calls for water and baptizes them immediately. The Jewish leaders of the Church are convinced by the story that ". . . God has granted life-giving repentance even to the Gentiles" (Acts 11:18).

Peter's speech is a typical recital of the essential preaching about Christ. He begins with the baptism of Jesus and concludes with his resurrection from the dead. Peter and all the disciples are now commissioned to bear witness to this good news, even, as Peter now knows, to the Gentiles.

The gospel reading for the vigil in Years A, B, and C is the empty tomb story from Matthew, Mark, and Luke respectively. Therefore, the gospel story for the Eucharist during the day is the empty tomb story from John.

All the Gospels agree that Mary Magdalene found the empty tomb. In the Gospel of John, she runs to tell Peter and the beloved disciple. Her key question is "Where?" She tells Peter, "We don't know where they have put him!" Later she tells the angels that she is weeping because she does "not know where they have put him." Supposing Jesus to be the gardener, she says, "Tell me where you have laid him." Magdalene is the most persistent seeker of the risen Christ. She is rewarded for her search by seeing him first.

Peter and the beloved disciple, meanwhile, have run to the tomb. John lets Peter go in first, thus recognizing his authority. Peter sees the burial wrappings, but apparently does not understand. The beloved disciple, however, image of the Church, sees and believes.

The passage from the Letter to the Colossians is an exhortation to live in the faith that our victory over death is already won. Christ has gone before us. In him we have already died. Therefore, nothing of this present life should worry us. Christ, who is now our true life, will come back for us so that we may share the glory he already enjoys. The victory is won; we await our share in faith.

Irene Nowell, OSB

Questions for Discussion

1. Why is Mary Magdalene an important figure in today's readings? Why is her search rewarded?

2. In what ways have you been involved in the Easter mystery this weekend? What touched you most deeply this year?

3. What does the Easter experience say to you about who God is in your life? In the world? In your parish?

For Journaling

1. I am seeking Jesus . . .

2. I have felt the absence of God . . .

3. I have found Jesus . . .

Second Sunday of
Easter

Witnesses to the Resurrection

Readings: **Acts 4:32–35; 1 John 5:1–6; John 20:19–31**

For the catechumens baptized at the Easter Vigil, the weeks after Easter are a time of *mystagogy,* a kind of
"honeymoon" period. This is a time to enter more deeply into the meaning of the new life of baptism. What
does it mean to live the new life of baptism *every day?* What does it mean to share life with these people
who make up the community of faith? As we welcome these new Catholics, we too reflect on what it means
to have died and risen with Christ in baptism. And we remember with gratitude those whose faith has
inspired us to open ourselves to this new life. Thus the readings for the Sundays after Easter spin out in
loving detail the effects of Jesus' resurrection. We retell the stories of Jesus' appearances after the
resurrection and reflect on the experiences of the early Church.

The sources used for Cycle B are primarily the Acts of the Apostles, the Gospel of John, and the First
Letter of John. The Acts of the Apostles is a second volume to the Gospel of Luke. It continues many of the
themes found in Luke. Both volumes have a particular interest in the Holy Spirit and prayer and an
attention to women, Gentiles, and outcasts. In the Gospel of Luke Jesus journeyed to Jerusalem. In Acts the
disciples travel out from Jerusalem "to the ends of the earth," that is, Rome.

In Acts there are three summary descriptions of the ideal Christian community. The community is formed
by faith in the resurrection and sent to bear witness to the resurrection (2:43–47, 4:32–35, 5:12–16). The
second summary, read on this Sunday, presents an ideal of the early Christian community. Those who were
committed to Jesus would belong to a community which would hold all things in common. Each would
receive what they needed from the common store.

Two examples, one positive and one negative, follow this description of the ideal. Barnabas, who becomes a
companion of Paul, sells a piece of property and contributes the proceeds to the community fund (4:36–37).
Ananias and Sapphira, husband and wife, also sell a piece of property. They contribute part of the
proceeds to the common fund, but pretend that the contribution is the total profit. Because of this
deception, each of them is struck dead (5:1–11). Thus we can see the real struggles of the community even
in the description of the ideal.

The second reading is from the First Letter of John. This letter was written by a member of the community
who gathered around the beloved disciple. It develops themes from the Gospel of John. The second section
of the letter, from which today's passage is taken, emphasizes the theme of loving one another. Today's
passage is written in the form of a chain, with each statement repeating a phrase from the previous
statement. The chain links together to form a circle with the statement of belief in Jesus the Christ (5:1), the
Son of God (5:5). The message of the circled chain is the profound truth that love of God and love of
neighbor are the proof each for the other. One cannot love God without loving God's children. On the other
hand, genuine love for God's children is proof of love of God.

The action which demonstrates this double love is the keeping of God's commandments. It is the children of
God who give and receive this love. The children of God are known by their faith in Jesus. This faith in
Jesus conquers the world. It makes possible the love of God and neighbor, which shows itself in fidelity to
the commandments. The possibility for this victory came through Jesus who died and rose to overcome the
death of this world. The victory is witnessed at the moment of his death by the blood, which shows him as a
sacrifice, and the water, which shows the gift of the Spirit. The Spirit gives witness to the truth of the
victory. The Spirit is given to believers in baptism into the death of Jesus, which gives them life as children
of God.

51

The gospel is John's description of the appearance of the risen Jesus to the disciples on Easter night (cf. Luke 24:36–49) and again a week later. The first appearance describes the gifts of the risen Jesus and his commission to the disciples. He gives them peace and joy, primary characteristics of risen life and of faith in the Risen One. He breathes new life into them as God breathed life into the first human creature (Genesis 2:7). He commissions them to reverse the alienation caused by sin (cf. Genesis 3–11) by forgiving sins. Risen life is characterized not by alienation but by love of one another.

The second appearance, also on a Sunday, emphasizes the necessity and the gift of faith. Thomas, a symbol for all who doubt, will not believe the witness of the other disciples. Jesus comes and again proclaims his gift of peace. Jesus demonstrates to Thomas by means of his wounds that he is indeed the same person. Thomas's answer is the strongest exclamation of faith in the Gospel of John. The appearance ends with a beatitude, proclaiming the happiness of those who believe only through the witness of the disciples. The final verses are the first ending to John's Gospel. They point out again the necessity of faith in the true witnesses to Jesus, the Christ, the Son of God.

Irene Nowell, OSB

Questions for Discussion

1. The ideal of sharing all things in common has not been lived often in the Church. Why do you think this is so?

2. What difference does your baptism make in the decisions of your daily life? In the way you spend your money? In the career you have chosen to pursue? In the way you vote?

3. Questions are a natural part of our growth in faith. What help does the story of Thomas have as you face the questions in your life?

For Journaling

"As the Father has sent me, so I send you."

1. I am sent by Jesus to . . .

2. My life was transformed this Lent when . . .

3. To me, faith is . . .

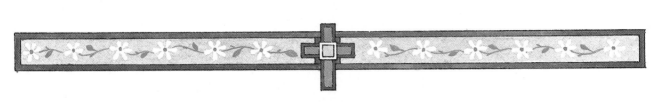

We Live a New Life

Readings: Acts 3:13-15, 17-19; 1 John 2:1-5; Luke 24:35-48

All we know of what it means to live a risen life is what we know about Jesus' risen life. He is the first to rise from the dead. His resurrection is the foundation of our faith that we too will rise again.

The stories of the appearances of Jesus after his resurrection give us our best revelation about risen life. In today's selection from the Gospel of Luke, we have Luke's version of the appearance to the Eleven. Last Sunday we read John's version of the same appearance.

In Luke there are two reports of earlier appearances: one which happened to two disciples on their way to Emmaus and the second to Peter. There are several significant similarities between the appearance on the way to Emmaus and the appearance to the Eleven. When Jesus appears to the Eleven, he eats and he explains the Scriptures, and then they recognize him in the breaking of bread. There is a message for us in Luke's description of Jesus' actions. We too find the risen Jesus in the Scriptures and in sharing a meal, especially in the sharing of word and food in Eucharist.

In both the Gospel of John and the Gospel of Luke, Jesus invites someone to touch him to see that he is not a ghost. The evangelists make every effort to tell us that Jesus' resurrection involves the whole person, body and soul. We assert in the Apostles' Creed: "I believe . . . in the resurrection of the body." Our bodies too, when they are transformed, are destined for new life.

Finally, as in the Gospel of John, Jesus greets the disciples with peace, his resurrection gift. In both Gospels Jesus commissions the disciples to preach forgiveness of sins. Forgiveness is a special interest throughout the Gospel of Luke. Now it becomes the heart of the disciples' witness. Risen life, won for us by Christ's death and resurrection, is a life of forgiveness and peace. We too, living the Christ life, must bear witness to Christ's peace.

Forgiveness is the message of the first part of today's selection from the First Letter of John (2:1-2). This first part of the letter centers around the theme that believers must walk in light because God is light. Walking in light, however, does not imply that one never sins. Rather, the believer is able to walk in light because Christ has become the "expiation for our sins" (2:2). Christ is also the Advocate who pleads our cause with the Father. He is the perfect intercessor. Christ is just; he lives in a totally loving relationship with the Father. He is the reverse of Satan, who is the Adversary making the case with God against us. (*Satan* in Hebrew means "adversary.")

The passage goes on to say that if we keep God's commandments we may be sure that we know God (2:3). In biblical terms, *to know* means "to experience." Thus keeping God's commandments will lead us to experience the presence and the life of God. Then, if we experience God, we cannot help showing God's presence in our lives. If we keep God's commandments, God's life will live in us. The essence of God's commandments is love of God and love of one another. Our participation in the risen life will be marked by love, forgiveness, and peace.

In the reading from the Acts of the Apostles, we have a section from a speech of Peter. Peter and John have just healed a lame man, and Peter is explaining the power by which they healed him. The power is the name of Jesus, the Messiah, who died and was raised to new life. This speech echoes themes from the Gospel of Luke, which is not surprising since both were written by the same author. The explanation from Scripture that the messiah would suffer is a new twist. The messianic texts had not been read that way before Christianity. Before Christianity, it was understood by many that the messiah would be a glorious king, bringing peace and prosperity. The early Christians, faced with the mystery of Jesus' death and resurrection, had to take a second look at those Scriptures. They came to understand that the kingdom was bought at the price of Jesus' death. His death brought the new life of peace and true prosperity, fullness of life.

Risen life was a wonderful mystery to the early Christians. They understood risen life only through experience of the risen Christ. They found him in the Eucharist, in the word, in their midst, bringing forgiveness, love, and peace. How do we ourselves understand the new life won for us in Christ?

Irene Nowell, OSB

Questions for Discussion

1. How do we bear witness to Jesus' gift of forgiveness? Do others see our parish community as a sign of Jesus' forgiveness?

2. Why do you think forgiveness is often seen as a sign of weakness rather than a sign of strength?

3. What situations in our world need our forgiveness in order for peace and healing to be present?

Journal Questions

1. What situations in your family need your acceptance and forgiveness in order for peace and healing to enter in?

2. For peace to happen in my life I must . . .

3. I am a witness to Jesus when I . . .

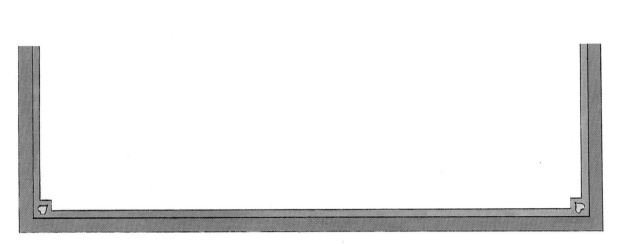

Fourth Sunday of
Easter

Following Jesus

Readings: **Acts 4:8-12; 1 John 3:1-2; John 10:11-18**

One of the chief messages of the resurrection is that Jesus is now the source of life and salvation. Only through following him will believers share in true life. As we ponder what following Jesus can mean for us today, we turn to the Scriptures to see what it meant for the early Church.

The reading from the Acts of the Apostles is a continuation of the reaction to the healing of a lame man by Peter and John. Last week we heard a portion of Peter's speech to the crowd who witnessed the miracle. Today we hear the story of the arrest of Peter and John. This is the first of several arrests for preaching Jesus' resurrection from the dead. Today's reading is Peter's speech to the authorities who are examining them. Through Peter, the basic truth of the resurrection is restated. Death has been conquered and life won through the death and resurrection of Jesus of Nazareth. In the name of Jesus, healing comes to the lame man; in the name of Jesus, salvation comes to believers.

Peter challenges the Jews by declaring that, although they share responsibility for Jesus' death, they must now put their faith in Jesus in order to be saved. (The Second Vatican Council made clear that passages like these are not to be interpreted to mean that the entire Jewish people are guilty for Jesus' death. It rejected the idea of a collective Jewish guilt. See *The Documents of Vatican II,* "Declaration on the Relationship of the Church to Non-Christian Religions," number 4, plus the footnotes by the editor. General editor: Walter M. Abbott, Jr. Chicago: Follett, 1966.) Peter quotes Psalm 118, comparing Jesus to the stone rejected by the builders which becomes the cornerstone. The response of the authorities to Peter's speech is amazement. After threatening the disciples with further punishment if they preach in Jesus' name, they let Peter and John go. Peter and John return immediately to preaching the good news, which cannot be suppressed, and all the people praise God.

A story of healing for which Jesus is challenged by the authorities also precedes Jesus' parable about the shepherd and his sheep. Jesus tells two parables at the beginning of John 10, one about the gate of the sheepfold and the other about the relationship between the shepherd and his sheep. Today's reading is the interpretation of the second parable.

Jesus describes himself as the ideal shepherd, one who will protect the flock, even at the price of his own life. He uses an image common in the Hebrew Scriptures or Old Testament, comparing the people of God to sheep. Ezekiel, for example, describes the plight of the flock at the hands of evil shepherds (Ezekiel 34). God announces at that time that he will shepherd the flock in order to nourish and protect them properly.

Sheep are difficult animals to care for. They take almost no initiative on their own behalf. In our eyes sheep sometimes seem helpless and stupid. We are not usually glad to be compared to them. But Jesus points out three characteristics of a shepherd which also characterize his relationship to believers. Like the sheep in this parable, we benefit from these characteristics of the shepherd.

First of all, the shepherd is genuinely devoted to the sheep. The shepherd is not like the hired hand who works only for pay. The shepherd serves the sheep. The shepherd protects the sheep even to death. Jesus, the shepherd, will lay down his life for the sheep. He lays down his life and takes it up again, just as he will lay down his garment to wash the disciples' feet and take it up again (cf. John 13:4, 12).

Second, the shepherd knows the sheep. He knows them not only intellectually, but at the level of life. He knows their habits and their needs. Jesus knows his sheep in the same way that he and the Father know each other. The sharing of life between Jesus and the Father is a model for the sharing of life between Jesus and believers.

Third, because the shepherd knows the sheep and is devoted to them, the sheep follow the shepherd. He calls the sheep by name, and they follow wherever he leads. Believers, in order to share Jesus' life and enjoy his protection, must follow wherever he leads.

We may not be happy with the image of ourselves as sheep. We should rejoice, however, in the shepherd who leads us. We can learn from sheep to trust in the shepherd's care and to accept the gift of his leadership without worry.

The reading from the First Letter of John is another description of the relationship between God and people. This section of the letter centers around the truth that believers should walk in light because God is light. But today's reading carries the idea even further: God has made us children through and with Christ. We are God's children. When we know (=experience) God face to face, we will be like God.

Our shepherd holds the gift of life. The life is greater than we can even imagine. All we must do is learn to follow well.

Irene Nowell, OSB

Questions for Discussion

1. Think of someone who has been a good shepherd for you. What qualities did that person have?
2. Even today, being a good leader can lead to imprisonment and even death. Name some modern examples.
3. How do we get to know Jesus, our Good Shepherd?

For Journaling

1. Walking in light means . . .
2. Following the Good Shepherd today means . . .

Vine and Branches

Readings: **Acts 9:26-31; 1 John 3:18-24; John 15:1-8**

Jesus is the vine; we are the branches. The image of growing things provides us another way to consider the risen life of Christ and our sharing in it.

The gospel reading from John is a meditation on Jesus as the vine and Christians as the branches. There are many vineyards in the area of Palestine, and the figure of the vine is common in the Old Testament. The prophets and the psalms describe Israel as a vine or vineyard planted by God (Psalm 80:9), flourishing (Ezekiel 19:10-11; Hosea 10:1), being pruned, bearing bad fruit, and being destroyed (Isaiah 5:1-7). Wisdom is compared to a luxuriant vine, nourishing all who partake of her (Sirach 24:17).

The image of Jesus as vine shares in some of the Hebrew Scripture or Old Testament ideas. Jesus, as the vine, is the source of life for his disciples. It is his life which lives in them. The disciples, as branches of the vine, are integrally united to Jesus and to each other. As a corporate unit, they form the vine. In Paul's image (Romans 12:4-5), they are members of the Body of Christ, branches of the vine which is Christ. Thus united, they are the Church, the new Israel. In the same image, Jesus himself is the new Israel.

If branches live in the vine, however, they must bear fruit. They are either fruitful or dead. There is no middle ground. A healthy vine must be pruned of dead branches in order to avoid disease. When new shoots appear, some must also be pinched off in order to make the remaining branches more fruitful. To live in Jesus, the vine, means that the disciple must bear much fruit. The only other alternative is death. The fire which awaits the cast-off branches may be the fire of judgment at the end of the world.

Risen life is not just given to us externally. It flows within us as the life of the vine flows within the branches. This shared life, of necessity, bears fruit in the vine. In our lives, the life of Christ of necessity results in good works, the work of Christ.

The selection from the First Letter of John declares the same truth without the image. If we truly love, if we truly live in God, we will love in deed as well as word. Our own judgment concerning how well we love is not the deciding factor. God's judgment is the deciding factor. Our task is to keep the commandments. Then God, who knows, will grant what we ask. Our task is to live with the life of Christ, to remain in him as the branch remains in the vine. We are able to do this through his life flowing within us, that is, through the Spirit given to us. This life will of necessity manifest itself in the works of loving one another.

As usual, the Letter of John presents us with a linked chain of truths, each dependent on the previous one and leading to the following one. Risen life has been given us in Christ. We must believe in Christ to share in that risen life. Sharing in that life will unavoidably lead to action, the action of loving one another, the action of good works.

The reading from the Acts of the Apostles narrates the consequences of Paul's conversion from being an ardent Jew to being a zealous Christian. The possibility of such a radical conversion seemed impossible to the other disciples. They feared a trick from their former persecutor. On the other hand, some of the Greek-speaking Jews with whom Paul debates seem all too ready to believe his conversion. They respond by trying to kill him. Only Barnabas takes Paul's side at the beginning. His influence leads to Paul's acceptance by the other disciples. The early Church had to learn the strength of God's grace and forgiveness at work in its midst. They had to learn to believe in the conversion of a former enemy. In the world of nature, we observe the mystery of growth and decline, of pruning and nurturing. From our observation, we learn about the mystery of growth in the Church, of growth in the risen life of Christ.

Irene Nowell, OSB

Questions for Discussion

1. In order to receive nourishment, the branches must remain attached to the vine. Tell about a time in your life when you especially needed nourishment from the Vine, the Church, the Body of Christ. How did you find that nourishment?

2. The vinedresser prunes the vine so that it can bear more fruit. What have been experiences of pruning for you? How did it result in your bearing more fruit?

For Journaling

1. I know God loves me because . . .

2. I know I love God because . . .

God Loves Everyone

Readings: Acts 10:25-26, 34-35, 44-48; 1 John 4:7-10; John 15:9-17

An ongoing human problem is dealing with those who are different from us, those who live in another country, those who belong to a different race, those who are not Christian, those who are not Catholic. The early Church faced similar problems. The first Christians were Jews. They had been trained rightly that they were the chosen people of God. To abandon Judaism was to abandon the covenant with God. To allow, and even encourage, others to worship God without following Jewish ways was heresy and scandal.

Last week we met Paul, who had zealously defended the principles of Judaism against the Christian "heresy." This week we find Peter struggling in the same conflict. Just before today's selection, Peter has had a dream. In it he is commanded to eat food forbidden by Jewish law. Horrified, Peter refuses. The command is repeated twice more. Then Peter is instructed not to call unclean what God has cleansed.

The vision prepares Peter for his meeting with Cornelius, a Gentile, considered by Jews to be unclean, a heathen. But as Peter begins to tell Cornelius and his household the good news of Jesus Christ, the Holy Spirit descends on all who are listening to him. Jewish Christians are amazed that the Holy Spirit would come upon Gentiles. Peter understands the event. He baptizes Cornelius and his household and declares that God shows no partiality but loves all people. When he returns to Jerusalem, Peter is called to give an account of himself to scandalized Jewish Christians there. After he tells the story, however, they exclaim: ". . . God has granted life-giving repentance even to the Gentiles."

We Gentiles find it surprising that the early Church did not recognize immediately that Christian faith should be open to Gentiles and/or that they should not be required to practice the customs of Judaism. How do we respond, however, to the possibility that God looks with favor on non-Christians or on Christians whose practices are different from our own? God shows no partiality.

The other two readings for this Sunday continue the instruction on the heart of risen life: love of God and love of one another. The story of Cornelius has added a new dimension to the exhortation about love. The love demanded of Christians must extend to all people. Their love must resemble the love of God, who shows no partiality.

The reading from 1 John is another chained series of statements which end with the crucial reminder: Love comes not from us but from God. It is God who loves us first. It is God who demonstrated the extent of love by sending His Son to give his life for us. Our love will always be dependent on God's love and modeled on God's love. Being able to love is a sign that we too are children of God; being children of God is what makes us able to love at all.

The gospel reading from John follows Jesus' description of the vine and the branches. The sign of life in the branches is the sharing in the love that flows between Jesus and the Father and between Jesus and the disciples. That love is all-encompassing. That love demands all we are, even to the point of giving up life for the sake of another. That is the ultimate keeping of the commandment to love one another. That love is demanded from us, not only for those who are like us, but also for those who are different. God shows no partiality, and it is God who is the source and end of our love.

Irene Nowell, OSB

Questions for Discussion

Anglican leader Robert Runcie, Archbishop of Canterbury and spiritual head of the state Church of England and leader of the world's seventy million Anglicans, has suggested that Protestants should come to give the pope some sort of primacy among Christians. Anglican leaders expect some kind of reunion between the Anglican and the Roman Catholic Church to be accomplished in the future.

1. What is the relationship between Protestants and Catholics in your town? What will need to happen before there can be unity between us? What changes will Protestants have to make? What changes will Catholics have to make?

2. Within the Catholic Church, there are people with wide differences of opinion. What ought to be our attitude toward our Catholic Christian brothers and sisters who see things differently than we do?

Journal Questions

The highlight of today's message is one of universal love. Just as God loves all peoples, so too are we to love everyone.

1. Who is someone you find it most difficult to love? Why?

2. How can you come to accept and love that person or that group as God has asked?

Or: To love unconditionally means . . .

Christ with Us

Readings for Ascension: Acts 1:1–11; Ephesians 1:17–23; Mark 16:15–20

Readings for Sunday: Acts 1:15-17, 20-26; 1 John 4:11-16; John 17:11-19

Departures are always difficult. Often they bring with them changes in status and responsibility. Spring is the season of graduations and weddings, each of which involves a departure and a change in relationships and responsibilities. At the time of the ascension, Jesus' disciples also found such changes along with his departure.

The only evangelist who tells the story of the ascension is Luke. He tells it twice, at the end of the Gospel and at the beginning of the Acts of the Apostles. Even his telling reflects the irrelevance of historical time for the risen Jesus who has moved beyond time. In the Gospel the ascension happens on Easter Sunday night; In Acts it happens forty days later. In the liturgical cycle, Year B is a problem on the Solemnity of the Ascension, since the Gospel of Mark is read in Year B and Mark has no story of the ascension. There are several later endings to the Gospels, however, which have been added to the original ending at Mark 16:8. The gospel read on this feast is from one of the later endings.

Our major source for the story of the ascension is chapter one of the Acts of the Apostles. Luke begins his narration of the early Church with the story of the ascension and the descent of the Holy Spirit. Jesus has remained with the disciples for some time as evidence of the resurrection, but now he returns to the Father. There are several important points concerning his departure. First of all, the disciples still think the kingdom will come in Jerusalem soon. Jesus says, in effect, that that is the Father's business.

Second, there is now a need for someone to carry on the work of Jesus in the world. That task falls to the disciples, led by the Twelve (representing the full number of tribes of Israel). Because of the defection of Judas, a replacement must be found to complete the number. The qualifications include being present with Jesus from his baptism to his ascension. The call is to bear witness to the resurrection. Following contemporary custom, the other disciples cast lots to choose the twelfth. The lot falls to Matthias, and he is numbered with the apostles.

Third, even though the number of disciples is complete, and even though their task is to continue Jesus' mission, there must be a divine presence among them. Jesus has departed and gone to join the Father. The disciples are instructed to await his promise. The fulfillment of the promise is the descent of the Holy Spirit, the divine presence who will remain with them, strengthening them to bear witness to the resurrection.

The gospel reading is from the last discourse in the Gospel of John. It is part of Jesus' prayer for his disciples. Jesus prays that they be protected by God's name and by God's word. They are guarded by God's presence. That presence has been given them in Jesus. God's word is truth, the truth that God sent His Son into the world to save it. This truth saves them from the Evil One. This truth consecrates the disciples. To consecrate means to set apart for some mission. The disciples are set apart from the world in order to be sent into the world to bear witness to Jesus, to continue his mission in the world.

The First Letter of John explains how the disciples continue the work of Jesus in the world. It is by loving one another. Love for one another continues God's presence in the world, because God dwells in those who love as God loves. The Spirit, which is the love between the Father and the Son, has been sent to remain with those who believe in Jesus. It is the Spirit in the disciples which bears witness to the truth of Jesus as Savior and Son of God. The most profound truths of Christianity are in the readings for this Sunday. God sent the Son to save the world; the Church continues his presence and mission in the world. How do we bear witness to the truth of our salvation?

Irene Nowell, OSB

Questions for Discussion

We are not just passing through life like a "paper fluttering in the breeze." Like the apostles, we are sent into the world by the power of the Spirit.

1. What is the role of the Church in bringing the message of God's love to all people?

2. How should the Church respond to issues that threaten the dignity and life of other human beings?

3. What should be the role of the Church in South Africa, in Washington, in Alaska, in New York, in any issue that threatens the earth and the environment?

4. What should be the role of the Church in our own town?

5. How does the Spirit speak to the Church today? How can we recognize the presence of the Spirit?

Journal Questions

1. What is my role in bringing the message of God's love to all people?

2. How does the Spirit speak to me?

3. I can be called a Christian when . . .

Pentecost

Empowered by the Spirit

Readings: Acts 2:1-11; 1 Corinthians 12:3-7, 12-13; John 20:19-23

Today is a beginning and an ending. It is the end of the Church's fifty-day celebration of Easter. It is the celebration of the beginning of the life of the Church in the world.

The story of Pentecost is told for us by Luke in the Acts of the Apostles. Luke has drawn out the Easter mystery with stories of forty days of appearances of the risen Christ and of his ascension. The story of Pentecost is set on the fiftieth day. The fiftieth day after Passover (50 = the day after seven Sabbaths) is the Jewish Feast of Weeks or Pentecost. Like Passover, it is a harvest festival. Religious significance was given to it by setting it aside as a celebration of the gift of the covenant Law on Mount Sinai. Pentecost is one of the three major pilgrimage feasts, and all Jewish men were expected to appear at the temple in Jerusalem, if possible (Leviticus 18:16-17). This explains the gathering of so many people in Jerusalem in the story in Acts.

The image of wind in the story recalls the exodus and creation. In the exodus a strong east wind dried up the sea so that Israel could escape. At creation a mighty wind swept over the waters (Genesis 1:2). Wind is related to breath. When God formed the human creature, God blew into it the breath of life. Thus the sound like a mighty wind at Pentecost recalls the creation of the world, the creation of the human being, and the creation of Israel as a people. This manifestation of the Spirit of God is the creation of a new people of God.

Creation originally was marred by sin and its consequences: suffering, separation, and death. One of the stories symbolizing the separation caused by sin is the story of the Tower of Babel (Genesis 11:1-9). The consequence of sin is the separation of languages. People can no longer communicate with one another. Pentecost, the final act of Easter, symbolizes the completion of our redemption. The separation caused by sin is overcome by the victory of Christ. Therefore, the disciples who are preaching this good news are understood by everyone in any language.

The Spirit of God appears at Pentecost not only as a sound like wind but also as tongues like fire. Fire is a common image for a manifestation of God. Two significant manifestations of God as fire are the burning bush which Moses sees (Exodus 3) and the fire and lightning at Mount Sinai at the making of the covenant (Exodus 19). Pentecost was already a celebration of the giving of the Law. Moses, of course, was a major figure in the making of the covenant. The fire at Moses's call links up with the fire at Mt. Sinai. Thus the tongues like fire at Pentecost symbolize a new call and a new making of the covenant. The new Law has been given, and the disciples are called to be its witnesses.

The gospel links this day with the beginning of the Easter season, since this passage was read also on the Second Sunday of Easter. The Gospel of John portrays the timeless events of Jesus' resurrection and the descent of the Spirit on the same day, Easter Sunday. The imagery is the same. Jesus breathes on the disciples, creating them anew, and proclaims the gift of the Holy Spirit. Jesus' resurrection gift is peace, sign of the new and risen life. Because they have been filled with this new life given in the Holy Spirit, they must do two things. Sent by Jesus, they must continue to spread the new life, and they must continue overcoming the separation caused by sin by forgiving sins. Paul in 1 Corinthians describes the unity of Christians who are filled with the Holy Spirit. They are one body, breathing with the same breath. The gifts of each contribute to the life of the whole.

Pentecost is a new creation, the gift of Christ's risen life. The separation of sin has been overcome; creation has been restored.

Irene Nowell, OSB

63

Questions for Discussion

1. What evidence can you see that the harmony and peace of God's creation is being restored in the world today?

2. How does the Spirit work through our parish to renew creation?

3. Where is reconciliation needed in our parish? In our community?

4. G. K. Chesterton said, "The Christian ideal has not been tried and found wanting; it has been found difficult and left untried." Do you agree?

For Journaling

1. I need the power of the Spirit to . . .

2. I feel the power of the Spirit when . . .

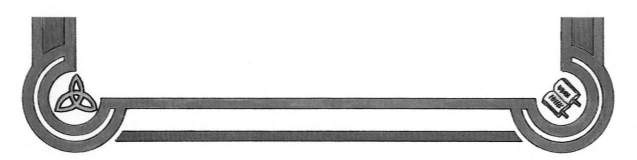

Three Persons in One God

Readings: Deuteronomy 4:32-34, 39-40; Romans 8:14-17; Matthew 28:16-20

The nature of God has always been a mystery for human beings. Our only way of explaining God must be through human images, and they are never sufficient. But God continues to reveal the divine nature to us throughout the ages. God longs to be known by us even more than we long to be known by God.

The seventh century B.C.E. author of Deuteronomy wrote for a people who had become complacent in their covenant life. He warned them of impending exile if they did not return to a lively faith in God. In this passage, through a speech of Moses, he describes the great care and concern of God for the people. The God of Israel is not like other gods, who live in a separate realm and care little for their people. The God of Israel is not removed from human history, but enters into history with great power to protect and save the chosen people. This God is the God of all creation. But this God desires passionately to be loved by this chosen people. This God desires to bless them and make them prosper. Therefore, the people must obey the covenant law. In this obedience they will find life with God. The persistent message in this passage is that God pays attention to people, that God cares for people and longs to be known by them.

The New Testament readings show the continuation of God's revelation to human beings. The greatest revelation of God is Christ. Paul, in the Letter to the Romans, describes this revelation in Christ. Jesus Christ is the true Son of God. Through Jesus, the Spirit—the shared life breathing between Father and Son—is given to human beings. This Spirit is not only a revelation of God: the Spirit brings human beings into a share in God's life. The same life breathes in Christians which breathes in God. Thus with Christ we become children of God, able to call God "Father." The revelation of God has moved from explanation to experience. *To know* in biblical terminology is "to experience." Through the Spirit we know God. We may not be able to explain our knowledge verbally, but our knowledge is much more intimate. We live with the life of God.

The gospel passage from Matthew is the last passage of that Gospel. It is Jesus' final instruction to the disciples after the resurrection. Jesus proclaims his authority over all creation. He then commissions the disciples to continue his work in the world. Finally, he promises to remain with his disciples until the end of the world.

The work which Jesus commissions the disciples to do is to continue bringing people to shared life with God. The way of Jesus defeated the power of Satan for all time and healed the separation from God caused by sin. The sign of this shared life is the gift of the Spirit, the shared life of the Father and Son. People are brought to this new life with God by being baptized into Jesus' death and filled with the Holy Spirit. Therefore, they are baptized in the name of the Father and of the Son and of the Holy Spirit.

This is the beginning of our knowledge of God. The fullness of God's revelation will come with the fullness of life in God's kingdom.

Irene Nowell, OSB

Questions for Discussion

1. Mystery is something which we experience in many different ways, but never find words adequate to describe. Think about the following experiences:

   When I witness a magnificent sunset or starlit sky, I feel . . .

   When the first drop of rain falls after a long absence of moisture, I feel . . .

   When I see the signs of love between an elderly couple, I feel . . .

2. How do words help you to express the mystery? In what way do they fall short?

3. Our understanding of the Trinity is more a matter of experience than of theological explanation. How do words help us to understand the mystery? In what way do they fall short?

For Journaling

The medieval mystic Mechtild of Magdeburg describes her experience of the Trinity as a "mother's cloak wherein the child finds a home and lays its head on the maternal breast." Does this image describe your experience of God? How would you describe the experience of the Trinity in your own life?

My favorite image of God is . . .

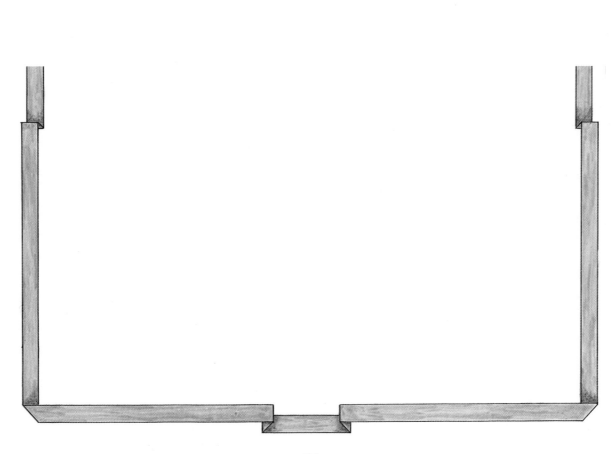

Corpus Christi
(Solemnity of the
Body and Blood of
Christ)

The Body and Blood of Christ

Readings: **Exodus 24:3-8; Hebrews 9:11-15; Mark 14:12-16, 22-26**

Blood is a primary symbol of life. Signs requesting donations to a blood bank say, "Give the gift of life." To be a blood relative of someone is to share life on a deep level. "Blood is thicker than water," we say. The Solemnity of Corpus Christi, the Body and Blood of Christ, has meaning on several levels. In Year B, the image of blood is used to help us understand the meaning of this feast.

The passage from Exodus is the story of the sealing of the Sinai covenant. Today when we seal a contract we do so with our signature, something which is a sign of our unique identity. No one may sign for us. We must leave a little of our life as a seal. The Sinai covenant was sealed with two ceremonies, each of which signified the sharing of life: a meal and a blood rite. The blood rite is performed to show that through the covenant God and the people have become blood relatives. The same blood is sprinkled on the altar, which stands for God, and on the people. Now God and the people have become one; they are family.

The sharing of blood always requires the shedding of blood. A mother bringing a child into the world sheds blood in giving birth. In order to show the shared life of the covenant, animals were sacrificed so that their blood could be used as a symbol.

The author of the Letter to the Hebrews points out that this was always an imperfect sign. The sprinkled blood of the covenant ceremony was not really the blood of either party, neither the blood of God nor of the people. Christ's death, however, provided the perfect sign. His blood, shed to reconcile and reunite human beings and God, was at one and the same time the blood of both covenant partners, human and divine. In Christ the shared life between God and human beings became incarnate. In himself he is the bond of the new covenant. God and the people have indeed become blood relatives.

The gospel tells the story of the sealing of the new covenant. Jesus celebrates the Passover supper with his disciples the night before his death. He seals the new covenant with a meal and with a blood rite. The cup of wine, the sacramental shared blood which seals the covenant, is shared with all the disciples. The blood which will be shed the following day is the sign of shared life between Jesus and his disciples. The covenant partners have become blood relatives.

A living covenant needs renewal. Israel held covenant renewal ceremonies from time to time. We celebrate covenant renewal every time we celebrate the Eucharist. The sacred bread and wine, the meal and blood, which we share, signify and effect the covenant life we share with each other and with God in Christ. The body and blood of Christ are the sign of the covenant life. The body and blood of Christ are the shared meal. The body and blood of Christ are the sacrifice which makes the meal and the covenant possible. We who share the Eucharist share Christ's life. We who share the Eucharist become the body and blood of Christ.

Irene Nowell, OSB

Questions for Discussion

At one time in the history of the Church, abuses led to the practice of having only the priest receive the Eucharist from the cup. Since we believe that Christ is alive, whole and entire, we believe that we receive the whole Christ when we receive only the Eucharistic bread. Since Vatican II, the full Eucharistic sign of the sacred bread and the wine have been restored to the laity.

1. Why is receiving from the cup in some sense a fuller sign of Eucharist? Why is it desirable for all to receive from the cup?

2. What qualities mark the relationship between blood relatives that cannot be expected of other relationships? What does it mean to be a blood relative to God?

For Journaling

1. I give my life for others when I . . .

2. I share in the Body of Christ by . . .

Jesus Conquers Evil

Readings: **Genesis 3:9-15; 2 Corinthians 4:13-5:1; Mark 3:20-35**

Finally on this Sunday the names of the two powers in the struggle come out. From the beginning of the Gospel of Mark, it has been evident that a battle is going on. Jesus claims authority which seems beyond an ordinary person. He defeats sickness and evil wherever he meets it. Now it becomes clear that the real conflict is between God and Satan, between the kingdom of God and the kingdom of evil.

The reading from Genesis is part of the primeval history (Genesis 1-11). In these chapters the Israelites tell the story of the creation of the world and explain why things are as they are. One of the greatest mysteries of life is the existence of sin and all its consequences—alienation, suffering, death. Today's passage is an explanation of why evil exists in a world created to be good.

Everything in the story is initially good. Even the clever serpent had been good. The fruit of the tree is good for many things—knowledge, beauty, nourishment. What is not good is the human inclination to turn from obedience to God to a reliance on human power and control. The human creatures decide to make themselves like God rather than to trust in God's creation of them.

The characteristics of temptation are evident in the story. There is distortion of truth on all sides. The serpent suggests that God will not allow eating of any fruit in the garden. The woman corrects that error but exaggerates God's prohibition to include even touching the forbidden fruit. The action is presented as good from all sides, and God is presented as desiring to harm human beings rather than to care for them. The fruit is seen to be good; eating the fruit is seen to be beneficial. The evil consequences are cleverly hidden by the clever serpent and the equally clever human beings.

But, as soon as the action is complete, the evil consequences emerge. The first consequence is separation of what belongs together. The human beings, made in the image of God, given life by the breath of God, hide from God. The woman, made from the flesh of the man, is abandoned by the man. The man ('adam), made from the earth ('adamah), is denied the fertility of the earth. Even the serpent is separated from all the other animals. The separation will grow throughout the rest of the primeval history. Brother kills brother, human violence causes a violent creation to threaten world destruction, human pride separates even human languages. The primary consequence of sin is separation and isolation. The ultimate separation is death, when even life is separated from the human being.

This is a description of the kingdom of evil, Satan's kingdom. It is characterized by sin, suffering, separation, and death. Jesus' miracles have been evidence that God has defeated the power of Satan. Jesus arrives announcing the kingdom which brings life, wholeness, and loving unity. The breath of God, the Spirit, is again blown into the human creature to make it live. But the scribes in the story can see only death. They accuse Jesus of defeating sin and death by the power of sin and death.

The point of the Christian message is in this gospel. It is not by Satan's power, but by God's power, that Jesus conquers evil. The domination of Satan, introduced into the world by human disobedience from the beginning of time, has been ended by radical human obedience, by the one person in whom alienation and separation find no home. Jesus is perfectly in tune with God, perfectly open to God's power and life, perfectly in God's image. His obedience restores the rest of humankind to God's image. The serpent said disobedience will make you like gods; Jesus says doing the will of God will make you children of God, his brothers and sisters.

The life of Jesus is the announcement of this good news. The gift of the Spirit is the pledge of the fullness of life to come, when there will be no more sin, suffering, separation, or death. That is what Paul describes for us in the passage from 2 Corinthians. We believe in the glory of God's kingdom whose fullness awaits us. The power of Satan is broken.

Irene Nowell, OSB

Questions for Discussion

1. If Jesus conquered the power of sin and evil by his death, why is there so much evil present in our world today?

2. Is there anything we can do to change the course of separation and isolation between people and countries? How does our faith and trust in God give us hope?

3. How do we bring God's love to those who are experiencing evil and the effects of evil in our world to day?

For Journaling

1. I see the power of evil in me when . . .

2. The power of the Holy Spirit is present in me when . . .

3. I resolve the conflict between good and evil in myself by . . .

The Kingdom of God Comes

Readings: **Ezekiel 17:22–24; 2 Corinthians 5:6–10; Mark 4:26–34**

On this early summer Sunday the liturgy directs our attention to growing things. Although growth happens without our causing or controlling it, we can have an effect on the conditions which allow growth to happen.

The prophet Ezekiel, who wrote during the Babylonian exile, tells several parables or allegories to illustrate the situation of the Israelites and the surrounding nations in the sixth century B.C.E. Chapter 17 is devoted entirely to the image of the cedar tree. The top of the tree is broken off and transplanted by a great eagle. The eagle than takes a seed, and when the seed is planted it becomes a vine. The vine reaches toward another eagle who transplants the vine. The vine is then threatened with rootlessness and death.

The image refers to Babylon (the first eagle) taking Israel (the cedar) into exile in 597. Ezekiel himself was in this group of exiles. Nebuchadrezzar of Babylon then appointed a puppet king, Zedekiah (the seed), to rule in Jerusalem. But Zedekiah turned to Egypt (the second eagle) for help. This resulted in a second attack by the Babylonians. Jerusalem was destroyed, Zedekiah blinded, his sons killed, and more people taken into exile.

God wants His covenant people to rely on Him alone. In today's passage we have the conclusion of the story of the cedar. God will take a shoot from the cedar and replant it in Israel. God will restore the exiled people, and they will flourish. Israel will become a shelter for all God's creation. This will happen, just as the exodus happened, so that all will know that Yahweh cares for His people (cf. Exodus 14:18). It is not major political powers that control what happens to God's people; it is God Himself who acts.

Jesus also used many parables to illustrate his message about the kingdom of God. Mark 4 is a collection of these parables. Two which refer to growing things are read today. Often a parable has only one point; the point is often unexpected and challenges the hearer to think differently. The first parable in today's gospel simply describes the process of growth. A farmer plants the seed and, then, when the time is right, harvests the crop. The growth happens without his causing it. Now we know that it takes much more work than that to grow grain. But Jesus is not talking about the farmer; he is talking about the miracle of growth. That is the one point of the parable. The point is that human power cannot make one grain turn into a full-blown, ripe plant. It is the power of growth in creation that does it. We may come to understand it. We may set the conditions. But it is the power of life that causes it to happen. So it is with God's kingdom. We may set the conditions, but the power of God causes it to produce.

The second parable centers around size, growth, and contrast. The mustard seed is a tiny seed, but the plant it produces is large. Just so the kingdom of God has small beginnings, but will grow out of all proportion to its tiny seed.

The purpose of a parable is to reveal something which is not known by means of a comparison to something which is known. With these two parables, Jesus uses the example of well-known facts about growing things to explore the mystery of the kingdom of God. For the advanced students, the disciples, he explains everything privately.

In the passage from 2 Corinthians, Paul points out that we do not always see the action of God, just as the farmer does not "see" the seed grow. But seeing is not important; faith is. Faith in Christ strengthens our hope that the kingdom is at work in us and in the world. We hope to nourish that growth so that we may be found ripe at the harvest.

Irene Nowell, OSB

Questions for Discussion

1. Many people view the kingdom of peace and justice as just a nice dream. What gives us hope for the coming of that kingdom?

2. What small steps are we taking in our family and in our parish to work with the kingdom of God? What gives us hope for this task?

3. As you look at the social and political situations in our world today, are you more likely to feel discouragement or enthusiasm? What hope do today's readings offer?

For Journaling

1. Faith in God's presence in the world allows me to . . .

2. Walk among the trees and let them speak to you of growth and change, of the mystery of God. Write your reflections.

God's Saving Power

Readings: **Job 38:1, 8–11; 2 Corinthians 5:14–17; Mark 4:35–41**

Storms are a convincing demonstration that there are powers in nature greater than our own. The people of the ancient Near East, who lived between the Mediterranean Sea and the Arabian desert, were regularly faced with earth-shaking storms. Their explanation for the creation of the world was based on the imagery of storms. According to the Canaanite myth, there was a battle between the storm god Ba'al and the sea god Yam. Ba'al won and set limits for the sea so that it could never overwhelm the dry land. But with the regularity of the seasons, the sea god attempts again to take over the land, and the storm god must again defeat him. So the myth of creation is re-enacted regularly.

When Israel told its story of creation, the people borrowed the Canaanite storm imagery. In the beginning there was a mighty wind over the waters (cf. Genesis 1:2). When God establishes the firmament, He divides the waters (Genesis 1:6–8). Then God collects the waters and sets limits for them so that the dry land may appear (Genesis 1:9–10). Israel also changed the myth: There is no battle. There is only one God. God is completely and calmly in control.

Throughout the Hebrew Scriptures or Old Testament, the Creator God is the one who rides the storm clouds and sets limits for the sea. When the author of Job wanted to describe the appearance of God to Job, he portrayed God as speaking from a storm. Job has been complaining that he does not understand the ways of God, that God is not fair. So God begins to ask him "godly" questions. He asks him ironically, "If you know as much as God, what do you know about creation?" One of God's first questions has to do with the creative act to hold the sea in bounds. Only the Creator can control the sea. Can Job do that? The result of God's questioning of Job is Job's realization that God is God and Job is Job. Job repents of his demands on God, and God restores his prosperity. Furthermore, God proclaims Job's questioning justified (Job 42:8). Job searched into things beyond him, the mysteries of creation and life, but Job has never doubted that God was in control and that God cared enough to listen to Job. And Job was right!

During the storm on the lake the disciples of Jesus seem to doubt. Throughout the Gospel of Mark, the disciples have difficulty understanding who Jesus is and what he is telling them. It is part of Mark's message that no one can understand Jesus as Messiah until after his death. So, in this incident, the terrified disciples—half in hope, half in despair—awaken Jesus. Their question seems to indicate that they think he can do something, but that they are afraid he won't. After Jesus calms the storm and the sea, they are astonished that he could do something.

In spite of their misunderstanding, they ask exactly the right question: "Who is this, that the wind and sea obey him?" It is similar to the question God asked Job. There is only one possible answer. Jesus must be acting in the power of the Creator God. No one else receives obedience from the wind and the sea. Jesus acts with God's power to defeat the forces of primeval chaos. In Jesus God brings the new creation to birth and defeats the powers of sin and death.

In 2 Corinthians, Paul preaches the wonderful news of the new creation. Not only is Christ a new creation, all who believe in him are a new creation, too. He died in the final battle with the powers of chaos. His resurrection is the final defeat of death. All of us share in his death by passing through the stormy sea of baptism. Through the creative word of God, whose Spirit-wind blows over those waters, we are brought to new life, new creation. The sign of the new creation is a new vision of life. Life is lived no longer for oneself, but for Christ. Christ died for us, we live for him.

Irene Nowell, OSB

Questions for Discussion

1. What efforts do we usually make to control the chaos that threatens us?

2. When you are afraid, where do you turn for strength?

3. What changes can take place when we let go and let God take control?

For Journaling

1. What frightens me most is . . .

2. When I am most fearful, I . . .

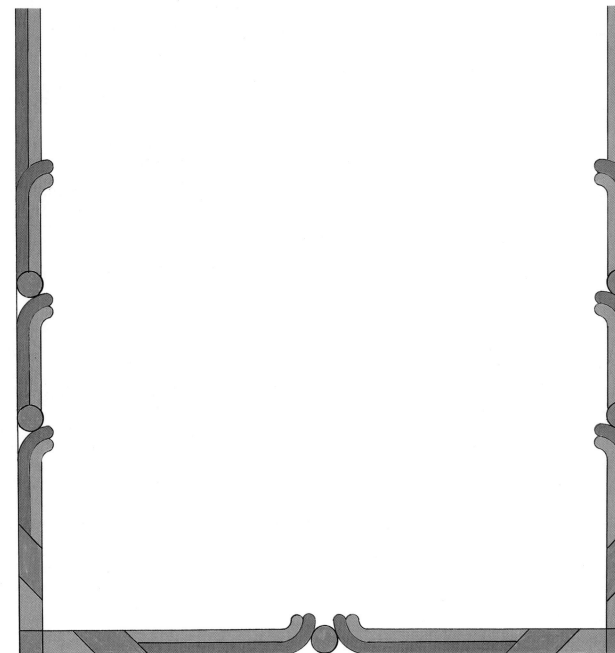

Life Is Precious

Readings: **Wisdom 1:13-15, 2:23-24; 2 Corinthians 8:7, 9, 13-15; Mark 5:21-43**

Throughout these Sundays after Pentecost the following theme recurs again and again: What is the meaning of suffering? What is the meaning of death? As we discussed early in the year, this was a great problem in the Old Testament. The author of Genesis and the Deuteronomic writers linked sin with suffering. It was a great insight, but not an answer for all cases.

Another group of writers, called the wisdom writers, spent much time pondering the mystery of suffering. They struggled to reconcile the mystery of suffering with belief in a just God. They came up with several partial answers. The Book of Proverbs and the Wisdom of Ben Sira (Sirach) continue to state that if you sin you will suffer. Sirach alludes to the fact, however, that this doesn't always happen. So he declares that God has the power at the moment of death to make things right, either by great suffering or great joy in that moment, implying that in the long run the good are rewarded and the bad are punished (Sirach 11:26). The author of Job says that the theory doesn't always work, but the wise Creator God is in control and cares for human beings. Qoheleth is sure the Deuteronomic theory is not the whole answer, but he continues to declare that it is better to trust in God anyway.

The problem all of these authors faced was explaining the mystery of suffering when there was no belief in life after death. We find it hard to imagine no concept of life after death, but the idea of resurrection began to emerge in Israel only in the last two centuries before Christ. After all, how could they begin to understand it before Christ's resurrection!

The only wisdom writer who begins to get a glimmer of faith in life after death is the author of the Book of Wisdom. He wrote in about 50 B.C.E. His first insight is that righteousness cannot die. In biblical language, *righteousness* always involves relationship, primarily relationship with God. Thus the author recognizes that the relationship with God, the shared life with God, cannot die. Therefore, the human being, made in God's image, cannot die.

Suffering and death are thus a distortion of creation. They come from the power of Satan. But Jesus' miracles are a sign that the power of Satan is broken and the kingdom of God has arrived. The gospel story for today presents two miracle stories sandwiched together. This is one of Mark's favorite techniques, to insert one story in the midst of another. That way each story comments on the other.

The miracle in the center of the story is the healing of the woman with the hemorrhage. It is a demonstration of the life-giving power present in Jesus and of the woman's faith. She simply touches him, makes contact with Jesus, and is healed. She had suffered for twelve years an affliction which rendered her unclean in the eyes of the law. One touch of Jesus' clothing and she is healed. The power of Satan is broken, new life has entered the world.

The other miracle is a resuscitation, a raising from the dead. The child is twelve years old. The father is the one who expresses faith. The professional mourners have begun their dirge. They and the other bystanders ridicule Jesus. But Jesus takes with him the parents and his favorite disciples and calls the dead child back to life. Jesus' authority over sin, suffering, and death has now reached its most complete expression short of his own resurrection, the total victory over death.

Irene Nowell, OSB

Questions for Discussion

1. Why do you think there is such a preoccupation with youthfulness in our society?

2. What do you think most people fear about getting older? About dying?

3. How does Jesus transform our understanding of death and mortality?

For Journaling

1. To be alive means . . .

2. Death to me means . . .

3. When I think about getting older . . .

Saints Peter and Paul,
June 29

Pillars of Faith

Readings: **Acts 12:1-11; 2 Timothy 4:6-8, 17-18; Matthew 16:13-19**

Today in a feast honoring Saints Peter and Paul, we celebrate the Church's apostolic foundation. We celebrate these two apostles together because they are twin pillars upon which the Church was built.

Peter was a simple fisherman when he was called by Jesus. Peter was the apostle who three times, the night before the crucifixion, denied knowing Jesus. Peter was the apostle who wanted to stay on the mountaintop with Jesus rather than face the dramatic changes that were to follow. It was Peter who walked on the water toward Jesus and who began to sink as he began to doubt the power of Jesus. This is the same Peter whom Jesus chose to be the foundation on which the Church would be built. Empowered by the Holy Spirit, Peter undertook the task of leadership, guiding the Church and strengthening his brothers and sisters in faith.

Paul's preparation for his life work was much different. He was a tentmaker by trade and a Roman citizen. He was a faithful Jew who had studied under the rabbi Gamaliel. Until his dramatic conversion on the way to Damascus, Paul (or Saul as he was called in Hebrew), had been zealously trying to wipe out the fledgling Church. Following his conversion, Paul became the apostle of the Gentiles, preaching the gospel to many non-Jewish communities around the Mediterannean Sea. Through his preaching and his letters, Paul championed these new converts and helped the Church to adapt and bring the good news to the non-Jewish world.

Both Peter and Paul had important roles in the development of the Church. Peter's was the role of direction and confirmation. Paul's role of preaching to the Gentiles sometimes led him to confront Peter as well as some of the Jewish Christians. But the stories of their confrontations at Jerusalem and at Antioch also reveal the common faith and inspiration that united them. Both Peter and Paul eventually came to Rome where they met martyrdom for their faith.

As we celebrate these two heroes of our faith, the readings selected for today would have us reflect on the power of God which worked through them. It is the same God who works in and through the Church today.

The first reading tells a story of God's power at work in the early Church. Preaching the message of Jesus was not an easy task for his followers. They faced opposition from their own Jewish people and from the Roman government. Today's first reading from the Acts of the Apostles reports some of those hardships. In an effort to contain and control the new teaching, Herod beheaded James, another apostle and leader of the Church in Jerusalem. Shortly afterward, on the feast of Passover, Peter was thrown into prison. Luke, the author of Acts, gives a dramatic account of how Peter was miraculously delivered while the Church was gathered at prayer. His deliverance happens with such ease that Peter thinks it is a "mirage," a dream. This event happened during Passover time, when the Jewish people celebrate their deliverance from slavery in Egypt. Luke would have us see in this another passover. The God who had given the Jews their freedom from slavery, had also given Peter the gift of freedom. This God would continue to deliver the Church.

The second reading is from the letter written by Paul when he was in prison for preaching the message of Jesus to the Gentiles. As he faces his own impending death, Paul writes to his close friend Timothy, recounting the struggles and hardships of his ministry. But even while facing death, Paul proclaims the power of God. He recognizes, with humility and honesty, that it was the presence of God in his life that gave him the strength to endure. He looks forward with hope to the gift that is yet to come.

In the Gospel of Matthew today, we hear Simon Peter profess Jesus as the Messiah. Peter, in the name of the apostles, recognizes Jesus as the Messiah, even though he does not fully understand what being the Messiah would mean for Jesus. Jesus tells Peter that this recognition is a gift, a revelation from the heavenly Father. Jesus names Peter the "Rock" upon whom the Church would be built. He entrusts the continuation of his ministry to this simple, bumbling man named Peter. He makes Peter the keeper of the "keys of the kingdom of heaven."

The celebration of these two early pillars of the faith is a celebration of thanksgiving and trust. We are grateful for all those ordinary and not so ordinary people who have been instrumental in bringing us to faith. And we trust that God will continue to guide His Church just as He did in its early years. Through the centuries, the Church has weathered many a storm. Despite persecution, dissension, and even corruption in its highest ranks, God continues to be with His Church. We can trust that Jesus will be true to his promise, "The jaws of death shall not prevail against it."

Jeanita Strathman Lapa

Questions for Discussion

We see two distinct aspects of the Church when we reflect on the lives of the two apostles, Peter and Paul, these "two pillars," the foundation upon which the Church is built.

1. What insights into the role of the Church can the lives and ministries of Peter and Paul offer us today?

2. How is the tension between Peter and Paul still present in the life of the Church? What obligation do we have to study, ponder, and challenge the Church?

3. How does the Church continue to shape the history of the world by its presence? How do we assist the leaders of the Church in the mission of bringing the message of Jesus to all people?

For Journaling

1. A person who is a pillar of faith for me is . . .

2. I am like Peter when I . . .

3. I am like Paul when I . . .

4. I have a responsibility in the Church to . . .

Finding God in the Ordinary

Readings: Ezekiel 2:2-5; 2 Corinthians 12:7-10; Mark 6:1-6

A part of the message of Mark's Gospel is that Jesus is not understood by those who know him best. Not only is it impossible to understand who he is as Messiah until he has suffered and died, it remains difficult for many to accept him at all because he is not what they expected. A major problem throughout the ages is accepting the word of God from unusual messengers. We have our own ideas of how God ought to act. When God acts in surprising ways, we are often tempted to reject it.

The prophet Ezekiel knew that to be a prophet was to expect rejection. In most of the accounts of the call of a prophet, the person called tries to escape the call, precisely because suffering and rejection are bound to come with the call. Ezekiel does not object to his call, but God tells him anyway that he will probably be rejected.

It would seem that Ezekiel would be an acceptable messenger. He was, after all, a priest. But messages concerning disaster are never easy to accept from anyone. Ezekiel acted out many of his messages in rather bizarre or provocative ways. He acted out the siege and destruction of Jerusalem by Nebuchadrezzar. He acted out the distress of the exiles of 587 B.C.E. His message was not welcome to many, nor was his bizarre behavior. But God had appointed him prophet, watchman for his people. Ezekiel had no choice but to proclaim God's warning of impending danger. Whether the people accepted his message or not, they would know that a prophet had been among them.

It would seem that Paul was not the ideal messenger either. He seems to have made enemies with his preaching and to have been somewhat abrupt in his speech. In addition, he had some affliction which he describes in today's reading from 2 Corinthians. He begged God to deliver him from his affliction, but God chose to allow Paul's affliction to remain. We do not really know what the affliction was; we do know Paul's response to it. Having begged God to remove his affliction, Paul is content with his weakness. He accepts his weakness with grace, recognizing that the power in his preaching is God's, not Paul's.

Paul teaches us a very important lesson. It is not easy to remember that our power for good comes from God. When we are successful, we like to believe that it is through our own talent and virtue. When we recognize our weakness, we are tempted to believe that we will necessarily fail. It is too easy to forget that in our weakness God's power reaches perfection.

On the other hand, even Jesus met failure. The people of his own hometown cannot see past the neighbor they knew. They think that they and their town are incapable of great deeds. Therefore, anyone who grew up there must be equally incapable. They are not prepared to accept God's surprise. They want the word of God to come according to their own imagination, not according to what is really God's plan. For that reason, Jesus is unsuccessful in Nazareth. His power, the power of God in him, is hindered because of the people's lack of faith.

If there is anything consistent about God it is that God is surprising. The ways of God are not human ways. The messengers of God do not look as we would have them look. The word of God does not always say what we would wish. Even when we are used by God as messengers, we do not have the gifts we think necessary. But, through all these unexpected ways, the power of God acts. We are called to be open and to believe.

Irene Nowell, OSB

79

Questions for Discussion

1. What is the message for us in the lives of the black South Africans, the child with Down Syndrome, the young man with AIDS, the armless man next door, the immigrant from Poland, or the young migrant worker?

2. Why is it often hardest to hear God speaking in the words of those who are closest to us, e.g., our spouse, our children, our elderly parent?

3. One way in which God continues His creation is through individuals, their lives, their words, their actions. We are "the eyes, the hands, the feet, the mouth of God." How do we use each of these senses to further the kingdom of God?

For Journaling

1. I am the eyes of God when . . .

2. I am the hands of God when . . .

3. I am the ears of God when . . .

4. I am the feet of God when . . .

5. I am the mouth of God when . . .

6. God surprised me when . . .

Evangelization

Readings: Amos 7:12-15; Ephesians 1:3-14; Mark 6:7-13

In the mystery of God's choice of us, other people are called to minister God's word to us, and we are called to minister God's word to them. This is not an easy mission, but it is an extremely important one. We become responsible for carrying God's good news to others.

The prophet Amos preached in the eighth century B.C.E. At that time God's people were divided into two kingdoms, Judah in the south and Israel in the north. Both kingdoms were enjoying a period of prosperity and seemed more interested in material gain than in the word of God. Even the priests at the central shrines in both kingdoms were servants of the kings and often protected the kings' interests before those of God.

Amos, a shepherd and tree trimmer in the southern kingdom of Judah, is called by God to preach in the northern kingdom of Israel. His primary message is that God will judge the chosen people even more strictly than the other nations. God will punish them for their wrongdoing even more because they are chosen. It is especially because they exploit the poor that they will be punished. Amos's message is, of course, not welcome. Amaziah, the priest at the northern shrine of Bethel, attempts to send Amos home to Judah. Amaziah is more interested in the king's favor than in God's word. But Amos responds by telling Amaziah that he is not a prophet by his own choice. It is not his own word that he preaches. It is God who called him and sent him to Israel; it is God's message he delivers. Whether Amaziah hears the word or not, it is God's message Amos proclaims.

In today's selection from Mark's Gospel, we find Jesus sending the Twelve out to proclaim the message he proclaims and to do the works he does. In Mark's summary of Jesus' activity in 1:34, we see Jesus healing the sick and casting out demons. The first message Jesus preaches is the message of repentance (1:14-15). Thus the disciples go out, sent by Jesus to do the work of Jesus.

This passage, however, immediately follows the story of Jesus' rejection in Nazareth. If Jesus is rejected, the disciples who are continuing his work should also expect rejection. This rejection must not deter them— there are too many others in need of the word of God. The disciples are instructed simply to leave the inhospitable place and to shake the dust from their feet in witness against those who reject God's word.

The first section of Mark's Gospel describes Jesus' authority over Satan and his works. From chapter six on, it becomes evident that this activity of Jesus causes a division among those who witness it. The works and words of Jesus divide believers from nonbelievers. The people of Nazareth do not believe Jesus. There will be others who do not believe the disciples whom he has sent. The growth of the kingdom occurs nonetheless.

On this Sunday a series of readings from the Letter to the Ephesians begins and will continue until the Twenty-First Sunday of the Year. The letter begins with a great hymn of praise to God for the choice of human beings. All people have been chosen by God in Christ, chosen even before creation. Jews were chosen first; Jewish Christians were the first to hope in Christ. Gentile Christians are now chosen, too, also redeemed by Christ and sealed with the Holy Spirit. This is the message preached by all who are sent by God to proclaim the good news in Christ.

Irene Nowell, OSB

Questions for Discussion

1. How do you think Amos must have felt preaching to the people of Israel who really didn't want to hear the message he had to preach? Who preaches this message today? How are they received?

2. Why is the mission of evangelization so difficult even today?

3. Why do most of us feel inadequate and fearful when called upon to share God's word with others?

4. How can we evangelize others by the way we live our daily lives?

For Journaling

1. I spread the message of God's love when I . . .

2. I am called to evangelize others by . . .

3. Think about people who have brought you the good news of Jesus. Write a letter telling them how grateful you are for this gift.

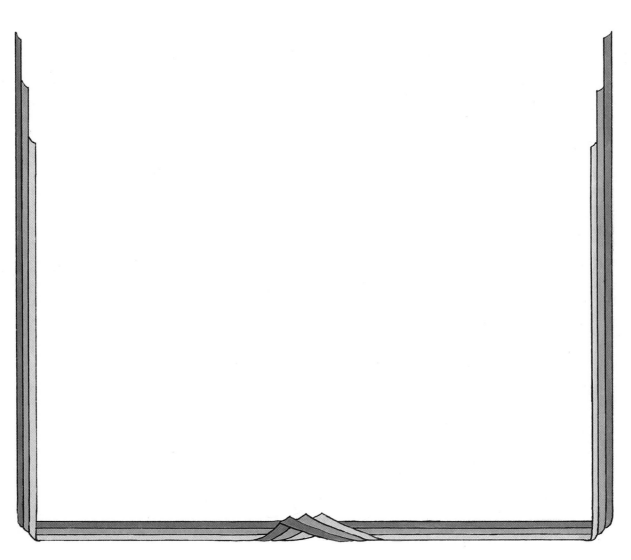

Sixteenth Sunday in
Ordinary Time

The Ministry of Leadership

Readings: Jeremiah 23:1-6; Ephesians 2:13-18; Mark 6:30-34

Even after the word of God has taken root in people, they need good leadership to guide and unite them as the people of God. God's covenant is not made with individuals, but with a united people. The leadership of that people is vitally important.

Jeremiah uses the favorite image of the shepherd to talk about the leadership of God's people. (See the similar passage by Jeremiah's contemporary Ezekiel in Ezekiel 34.) Jeremiah preached in the sixth century B.C.E., just before the Babylonian exile. He attempted to warn the people that, unless they turned from their evil ways and returned to God, they would lose the land and be driven into exile.

In great part, Jeremiah blamed the leaders of the people for the current distress. He compares them to shepherds who have not cared for the sheep. Rather than unite them, these shepherds have scattered the sheep. God then proclaims a solution: God will become their shepherd. God will unite them and nourish them. God will appoint good shepherds for the sheep.

The shepherd image is important for the growing messianic hope, the hope for a king like David. David had been a shepherd in his youth; David had been a good king who had united the people and established peace and prosperity. His name, "The Lord our righteousness," indicates that Jeremiah may have thought Zedekiah (= the Lord our righteousness) might be this good shepherd.

Initially Jeremiah's message seemed to be a failure. The people did not turn from their evil ways. They and Zedekiah, their king, were taken into exile. There seemed to be no good shepherds. But the leaders of the people in exile saved the words of the prophets and used them to nourish hope in the future. They proclaimed God's fidelity. The promises of God might not be fulfilled at the moment and in the way we expect, but ultimately God's promises must come to pass. In such a way, the leaders of the exiled people, as good shepherds, kept the people united and nourished them with hope.

Jesus sees the people of his day as being sheep without a shepherd. They lack strong leadership and are scattered. They are hungry for the word of God which Jesus brings them. The disciples, who have just returned from their first missionary journey of ministering to those people, think that they will get a well-deserved rest. But the hunger of the people overrides the disciples' need for rest. Jesus, the Good Shepherd, cannot resist the need of the sheep. There is no word of the disciples. Perhaps, while the disciples rested, the Master took over. Perhaps there is a message there for us, too.

The author of the Letter to the Ephesians continues the discussion about those who have been chosen in Christ. He points out that natural divisions are not long relevant. He will eventually conclude that all who are called in Christ are one body (Ephesians 4:4). In this passage he is emphasizing the unity between Jews and Gentiles, those who have seemed to be separated throughout the ages. Christ, through his death and resurrection, has created one new human being in himself. All who are redeemed through his cross are one body in him. Old enmity means nothing; Christ has become our peace. No shepherd could create greater unity; no shepherd could nourish his flock with greater peace and prosperity.

Irene Nowell, OSB

Questions for Discussion

1. What qualities do all good leaders have in common?

2. What lessons do today's readings offer to leaders? To followers?

3. How do the leaders in the Church continue to proclaim God's promise of salvation to all people?

For Journaling

1. I am a leader when . . .

2. When people do not want to follow my lead, . . .

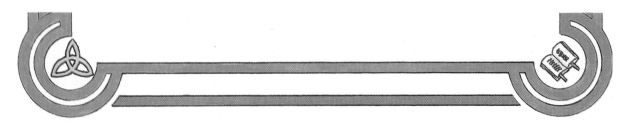

Eucharist as Meal

Readings: **2 Kings 4:42-44; Ephesians 4:1-6; John 6:1-15**

Eating together is one of the most significant of human acts. It is our favorite way to celebrate. Whoever heard of a party without something to eat and drink? Think of Thanksgiving or Christmas or the Fourth of July, a wedding or a birthday, without something to eat, without eating together. Somewhere in the center of our being, we know that eating together means more than simply nourishing our bodies. Somehow we know that to eat together is not only to share what nourishes our life, but to share life itself. Because eating together signifies sharing life, being left out of a meal signifies separation from that shared life. Running out of food is a terrible thing, not just because people will starve, but because they are prevented from sharing.

The prophet Elisha faced this disaster of insufficient food. Elisha, a ninth-century prophet, had gathered a group of prophets around him. They live a sort of communal life, sharing all things. When someone brings a gift of food, there is consternation because it won't feed everyone. Elisha insists that everyone will be fed. Indeed, not only is everyone satisfied, there are leftovers. Elisha's action signifies that the shared life of the prophets nourishes each of them. Not only does it nourish them, there is an overflow of life to nourish others. The true nourishment of the prophets is God's word. The life of God's word nourishes all around them.

The gospel is John's story of Jesus' multiplication of the loaves, a miracle similar to that of Elisha, but with even greater significance. For the next five Sundays, the liturgy leaves the continuous reading from the Gospel of Mark and turns to the Gospel of John. The story at this point in the Gospel of Mark is the multiplication of the loaves and fish (Mark 6:35-44). John's Gospel, however, has not only the story of the multiplication, but also Jesus' discourse explaining the significance of the miracle. For this reason, the Gospel of John is chosen for the next several Sundays.

The basic outline of the miracle story of the multiplication of the loaves is the same in all its occurrences (Matthew 14:13-21, 15:32-39; Mark 6:35-44, 8:1-10; Luke 9:11-17; John 6:1-15). A large crowd gathers around Jesus. The place is deserted. There is neither place nor money enough to feed the crowd. A small number of loaves and fish are discovered. Jesus asks the disciples to prepare the crowd. He blesses and breaks the loaves. Then he asks the disciples to distribute the food to the crowd. There is not only enough; again there are even leftovers! In the Gospel of John the people who have seen the miracle decide that Jesus is a messianic figure and rush to make him king. If he is king, there will never be hunger again!

The early Christians recognized in this miracle what the observers recognized in the Gospel of John. Jesus is the Messiah, and if he is king, there will never be hunger again. But they recognized it on a different level. The kingdom of Jesus is not a political kingdom, but the kingdom of God. The hunger that will be satisfied is not the hunger for today's nourishment, but the hunger for salvation. The meal that will satisfy that hunger is the Eucharist, the meal at which Christians, by sharing the sacred bread and wine, share life with Christ and with each other.

Recognizing this parallel, the early Church used the vocabulary of the multiplication story in its Liturgy of the Eucharist. Jesus "takes," "gives thanks," "gives." The Greek word for the fragments left over, *klasma,* became the common term for Eucharistic bread remaining after the celebration. It is interesting also to note that the Gospel of John has no Eucharistic narrative. The multiplication of the loaves becomes the symbol for Jesus' Eucharistic feeding of his disciples through the ages.

The unity given to Christians through the shared life of Eucharist is the subject of today's passage from the Letter to the Ephesians. Christians are indeed one body in Christ, joined in baptism, children of one God. This unity must be lived in their actions—peace, patience, humility, love. We share one meal, we share one life.

Irene Nowell, OSB

Questions for Discussion

1. What happens inside you when you share a meal with someone you love? What feelings are stirred within you? Is it the food you share, the place, the lighting, the silence, the music, or the conversation that is most important?

2. How is this meal like the meal you share at the Eucharist? Where does the comparison fall short?

3. How does the story of the prophet Elisha help us to understand the meaning of the Eucharist?

4. What are we asked to bring to the Eucharistic celebration? How can we feed all the hungry in our world?

For Journaling

1. Whenever I share a meal with a loved one, I am reminded of . . .

2. I share my own body and blood in Christ in the Eucharist by . . .

Eighteenth Sunday in
Ordinary Time

Bread of Life

Readings: **Exodus 16:2–4, 12–15; Ephesians 4:17, 20–24; John 6:24–35**

During this late summer season, the Church continues to look at the fruit of the harvest, bread. This primary human need for nourishment reveals on another level the primary need for the Bread of Life.

The community of Israel spent forty years (a number symbolizing a long time) in the desert between the exodus from Egypt and the entrance into the Promised Land. The forty years are characterized by endless murmuring, murmuring about food, murmuring about water, murmuring about leadership. Today's reading is found very shortly after the story of the miracle at the sea. Already the people have forgotten God's care for them at that extremely vulnerable moment. They have escaped the Egyptian army; now they fear starvation. Immediately, the focus of the grumbling becomes the leader, Moses. Immediately, hated Egypt looks better than the unknown desert, and they wish to undo the exodus.

God, however, is very patient with this cantankerous group. In every story of grumbling in which there is genuine need, God provides for the people. Only in the stories where there is no need does God become angry with them. In today's story there is genuine need; thus God provides both bread and meat.

There has been much discussion concerning the nature of manna. It is commonly assumed to be a secretion from the tamarisk tree. But the point of the story is not the kind of food, but rather that God has provided for the people at this moment when they are totally dependent. God nourishes them so that they may know that Yahweh is their God. For the same reason, God sent the plagues and parted the sea—so that they might know that Yahweh is their God (cf. Exodus 7:5, 8:22, 10:2, 14:18). God is present to the people in their need. God sustains their life.

Today's gospel begins the discourse in which Jesus explains the miracle of the multiplication of the food. Between this passage and last Sunday's story of the multiplication is the story of Jesus walking on the water to join the disciples who are crossing the Sea of Galilee. That is the point of the crowd's question to Jesus, "How did you come here?" Jesus uses the question to lead into his explanation of the miracle of multiplication.

The discussion turns on the meaning of "sign." Jesus scolds the crowd because they do not understand the signs. Then they ask for a sign. The common purpose of a sign is to convey a message. Traffic signs, posted announcements, name plates on doors, all have the purpose of conveying information. The same is true of biblical signs. Signs in Scripture convey the message that the power of God has broken the power of Satan. The manna in the desert conveyed the message that Yahweh was true to the name, "I am with you." Jesus scolds the crowd because they are more interested in the sign itself than in the message. The manna was a sign of God's presence, the true nourishment of the community's life. Jesus' multiplication of the loaves is a sign of Eucharist, a sign of God's presence in Christ. Jesus, Bread of Life, is the true nourishment of the community's life. The crowd has focused on the sign and failed to believe its message.

The continued reading from Ephesians emphasizes that Christians live life on a new level. They have become a new creation in Christ, and now they must think in a new way. The crowd to whom Jesus spoke in the Gospel of John needed this new way of thinking. A true sign should lead to new understanding. The need for nourishment to sustain life becomes a sign of our need for the presence of God to sustain our lives forever.

Irene Nowell, OSB

87

Questions for Discussion

1. In what ways do people today tend to focus on signs, rather than on the message?

2. How is bread a sign of the covenant of love made with God's people?

3. God is present in all human needs. What experiences in your life reveal this truth?

For Journaling

1. To me bread is . . .

2. A sign of God's love for me is . . .

God Is with Us

Readings: Daniel 7:9-10, 13-14; 2 Peter 1:16-19; Cycle A: Matthew 17:1-9, Cycle B: Mark 9:2-10; Cycle C: Luke 9:28-36

Throughout our lives there are certain "peak" experiences when we are keenly aware of the presence of God. Perhaps something has made us particularly conscious of God's care and concern for us. It may be in a moment when we realize that a prayer has been answered, or it may be simply in a moment of quiet reflection. We find ourselves overwhelmed in the face of God's great love, and we may even sense that we have glimpsed a little of the great glory of our God.

The transfiguration was such an experience for the disciples who went with Jesus to the mountain. It was a time of "glimpsing" the glory of God as manifest in Jesus, God's Son. It was a time of being strengthened for the road which lay ahead.

The story of the transfiguration is recounted in all three of the Synoptic Gospels. (Matthew, Mark, and Luke are known as the "synoptic" Gospels. They "see" and present the story of Jesus in a similar manner.)

The glory of Jesus was revealed in his ministry, healings, and teaching. It was revealed fully in his resurrection. And it was revealed in a special way in the transfiguration to confirm what he had just taught the disciples about the fact that he must suffer and die. The transfiguration revealed who he really was: the beloved Son of the Father.

The Gospels depict Jesus as frequently withdrawing by himself to pray (Luke 3:21, 6:12, 11:1). Undoubtedly, the mountaintop experience of the transfiguration reflects those times of shared communion. In these times of prayer, Jesus received assurance about the mission which God had entrusted to him. In these times of prayer, Jesus received the strength to continue on the way to Jerusalem.

In the event recounted in today's gospel, the disciples receive assurance and strength to continue that journey with Jesus. The disciples are Peter, James, and John, who are frequently singled out in the gospel as privileged recipients of certain teachings or as witnesses of certain miracles (Mark 1:29, 5:37-38, 14:33). One might think of them as a certain "inner group" among the disciples, whose privileges entailed certain responsibilities (and indeed after the resurrection, they were leaders in the early Church).

In the biblical setting of today's gospel, Jesus' final journey to Jerusalem, Peter has just professed that Jesus is the Messiah (Mark 8:29; Matthew 16:16; Luke 9:20). For some of the disciples, this realization may have had political connotations as well. Some of the Jews expected a political messiah who would liberate Israel from its enemies (Romans) and inaugurate a time of national independence. Jesus is quick to explain that this is not the nature of his messiahship. His way, or rather, the way of his Father, will involve suffering and death (Mark 8:31, 9:31, 10:33-34; Matthew 16:21; 17:22-23, 20:18-19; Luke 9:22; 9:44, 18:31-33). Even though Jesus spoke of his resurrection as well, the disciples did not understand what he meant. The transfiguration then follows to support the authority of what Jesus had just taught.

The appearance of Moses and Elijah, who represent the Law and the prophets, points to Jesus as the fulfillment of all that had been foretold in the Scriptures. Besides his association with the Law, Moses typifies the whole passover/exodus experience of Israel. In the Gospels the suffering and death of Jesus are depicted as a new passover event: Jesus passes over from death to life. (Recall too, that for the Synoptics, the Last Supper is portrayed as a celebration of the meal of Passover—Mark 14:12-26; Matthew 26:17-35; Luke 22:7-38; cf. Exodus 12.) In the Lucan account of the transfiguration, Moses and Elijah speak with Jesus about his passage (or "exodus" in the Greek text) in Jerusalem.

In addition to associating Moses and Elijah with the Law and the prophets, Jewish tradition believed that both Moses and Elijah had been mysteriously taken up into heaven. (Cf. 2 Kings 2:11-12; Deuteronomy 34:6). Accordingly, the account of the transfiguration hints at a similar "end" for Jesus. On the other hand, the uniqueness of Jesus in the history of salvation is pointed to by the fact that Jesus is described as fulfilling what Moses and Elijah represent (the

Law and the prophets), by the fact that Jesus alone is called by the Father "My Son, My Chosen One" (implying Messiah also), and the fact that Jesus stands alone at the end of the revelation.

The belief that the crucified and risen Jesus was taken up into heaven and exalted is the reason that the passage from Daniel is chosen for today's first reading. The reading recounts a vision given to the prophet, in which he sees the heavenly throne of God (the Ancient of Days). The reading abounds in images associated in apocalyptic literature with the heavenly sphere: the color white, brightness, radiance, streams of fire, myriads of angels. (Apocalyptic literature is a type of literature dating from 200 B.C.E. to A.D. 100. It includes the Book of Daniel as well as writings not found in the Bible. The word *apocalypse* comes from a Greek word meaning revelation. The contents of the writings result from some special revelation mediated to a person by an angel. Highly symbolic language and imagery is used in the writing. See for example, the Book of Revelation in the New Testament.)

Of particular interest in terms of today's feast is the second part of the reading from Daniel, which describes one who is "like a son of man." In its most basic meaning, "son of man" means a human being. (For example, the prophet Ezekiel is addressed as "son of man" throughout his book.) The human figure in Daniel, who perhaps represents the chosen people as a whole, is exalted by God, while the enemies of God, "the beasts" in verse 11, are destroyed.

In the Gospels "Son of Man" is a title which is applied to Jesus. Drawn from Jewish tradition, the title refers to a human being who is rewarded for his righteousness and exalted by God. In the Gospels it is a messianic title. The figure in Daniel is a kingly figure, whose dominion is forever. In the Gospels Jesus is mockingly crucified as king of the Jews (Matthew 27:37; Mark 15:18; Luke 23:38), but he is exalted in heaven as King of Kings (Revelation 17:14). It can be said that Jesus combined the image of the triumphant Son of Man with the image of the Suffering Servant of the Lord.

Caught up in the glory which Jesus manifests in today's gospel, the disciples want to stay there forever. But today's gospel affords only a peek at Jesus' full glory and final victory. For now there is the journey which lies ahead. "This is my Son, listen to him." His message entails a way of the cross. It is a way through death to life, as he had taught them.

The experience of Jesus' transfiguration is meant to strengthen not only the disciples, but also those to whom the words of the disciples later come. It is in this light that the author of the Second Letter of Peter can share the experience with the Christians of his own day. The writer is fortified and in turn fortifies his listeners by the story of the transfiguration. He emphasizes that the account of the revelation of Jesus' glory is not something which is made up; it is real, rooted in the experience of those who journeyed with him. Our own liturgical experience of the transfiguration and other peak experiences can fortify us. On the "mountain" one finds a ray of light which illumines the darkness preceding the dawn of his coming at the end of time. Here one finds direction and strength for the journey ahead. It is a journey which leads through suffering to life. It is a journey on which he was gone before us.

"This is my Son, my beloved, listen to him."

Anne Marie Sweet, OSB

Questions for Discussion

1. John Dunne speaks of the journey to God as a "journey from the mountaintop to the marketplace and back again." What do you think he meant? Is this your experience?

2. Why were the disciples confused about who Jesus was? Is the world still confused? Why or why not?

For Journaling

1. A time when I felt overwhelmed by the presence of God was . . .

2. I feel closest to God when . . .

3. One thing that sustains my faith is . . .

Sharing God's Life

Readings: **1 Kings 19:4-8; Ephesians 4:30-5:2; John 6:41-51**

The sign of the food, of shared life, of God's nourishment of creation, is so powerful that again this Sunday we attempt to probe its meaning. Many of the ideas that emerged in previous Sundays reappear in the readings for this Sunday.

The story from 1 Kings is part of the cycle of Elijah-Elisha stories. Several chapters in 1-2 Kings are devoted to wonderful stories about these two ninth-century prophets. In today's story Elijah has just come from a contest with the prophets of Ba'al in which he successfully demonstrated that Yahweh, not Ba'al, is God in Israel. Queen Jezebel, however, was devoted to Ba'al. Elijah has slaughtered all the priests of Ba'al as false prophets. Jezebel, therefore, is pursuing Elijah to kill him.

The fleeing of Elijah is desperate. His mission seems unsuccessful; he fears for his life. So he flees into the desert and prays for death. God's answer to his prayer is a kind of re-enactment of the exodus/desert experience of Israel. An angel feeds Elijah with bread and water just as God fed the Israelites with bread and water. Strengthened by that food, he walks forty days and nights, just as Israel wandered forty years. His destination is Mount Horeb, which is the same as Mount Sinai, the central stopping place for Israel and the scene of their covenant-making with God.

Elijah flees into the desert, a discouraged, desperate man. He is transformed by the bread and water sent from God. After God feeds him, he travels resolutely on a pilgrimage to the central shrine of the covenant. There he will receive from God a new commission which will change the political life of three countries: Judah, Israel, and Syria. He is a new man.

The gospel reading continues the Bread of Life discourse from John. Just as Israel murmured in the desert about food and water and leadership, those who have seen the miracle of the loaves murmur about Jesus, the Bread of Life. He cannot be a true leader sent from God because they know his parents! How can he give his flesh to be the Bread of Life?

Just as God was patient with Israel in the desert, Jesus patiently explains the meaning of his words to the crowd. He makes two major points: The purpose of nourishment is to sustain life. Shared nourishment signifies shared life.

First of all, the purpose of nourishment is to sustain life. But every food they have known, even the manna God sent in the desert, has sustained life only temporarily. Eventually death came. The bread which Jesus is will sustain life forever. There will be no more death. The one who eats this food will live forever.

The second point explains the first. If to share food is to share life, then to share this Bread of Life is to share life with Jesus. Jesus shares life with the Father, and that life is everlasting. Even though Jesus dies, the Father raises him to life again. Thus to eat this bread is to share in God's life which lasts forever. This food transforms human life into shared life with God.

The Letter to the Ephesians continues to describe this new life shared with God. Christians who live by this new life must be like God whose life they share. God is forgiving; they must forgive. Christ gave his life for love of us; we must in turn spend our lives for love. The sins which separate us—bitterness, anger, harsh words—must find no place in those who share God's life with one another. This shared life is symbolized and renewed in every Eucharistic celebration as we share again the food which transforms us.

Irene Nowell, OSB

Questions for Discussion

1. How does God continue to transform His people through the Eucharist?

2. How does God continue to transform the faith of a community?

3. When a parish in Minnesota was divided because of misunderstanding, bitterness, and anger, the local bishop refused to let them have Mass in their parish. What reason for this action can you see in today's readings?

4. The early Christian community believed that when they shared food with anyone, they also became responsible for that person. How is this true of the Eucharist?

For Journaling

1. My life has been transformed most by . . .

2. Transformation for me means . . .

Jesus Is Present in the Eucharist

Readings: **Proverbs 9:1–6; Ephesians 5:15–20; John 6:51–58**

This is the season of picnics and backyard barbecues, weddings and reunions. As we celebrate our joy in life together with the gifts of the summer, the Church gives us two more Sundays to ponder the theme of eating.

The Book of Proverbs presents a scene in which two women invite the passersby to a banquet. Lady Wisdom and Dame Folly call out similar invitations. The consequences of accepting one or the other, however, are vastly different. Eating with Dame Folly leads inevitably to death; sharing Lady Wisdom's meal is a guarantee of life. Those who are invited are the same: the simple and those who lack understanding. They are separated by accepting one or the other invitation. Those who are willing to take in what Wisdom offers have already made a wise choice. Their experience that Wisdom gives life will encourage them to continue sharing in her banquet.

The gospel continues Jesus' invitation to the banquet in which the food shared is his flesh and blood. This last section of the Bread of Life discourse becomes disturbingly graphic. Jesus offers literally his flesh to eat as real food and his blood to take as real drink. In addition to ordinary human revulsion at such an idea, the suggestion seems to fly in the face of Jewish law. Kosher meat is slaughtered in such a way that most of the blood is drained. The blood is regarded as the evidence of life, and life belongs to God alone. The listeners, hearing that they are to drink his blood, were scandalized. In addition, the word used for *eat* is a crude term used often for animals eating. It is no wonder they quarreled among themselves.

Jesus, however, makes no attempt to soften his words. The mystery of the Eucharist implies a real sharing of his flesh and blood as food, a real sharing of his life as nourishment. The giving of his flesh, which suggests his death, will provide believers with the food for eternal life. To share his life is to share the life of God, who sent this food from heaven to sustain the people. Choosing to share in the banquet Jesus offers seems on a human level to be foolish. The choice, however, is the wise act that leads to life.

The Letter to the Ephesians, after encouraging us to live wisely according to the will of the Lord, exhorts us to praise God for the wonderful gift we have been given. We share in God's life, we share the food which sustains that life forever.

Irene Nowell, OSB

Questions for Discussion

1. Have you ever tried to explain the mystery of the real presence of Jesus in the Eucharist to a nonbeliever? What did you say?

2. What does *wisdom* mean to you? Who are wise persons you know? How do these persons fit the descriptions given in today's readings?

3. How has your understanding of Eucharist developed since you received your First Holy Communion?

For Journaling

1. Lady Wisdom invites me to . . .

2. Dame Folly invites me to . . .

3. A wise person is one who . . .

Eucharist: A Covenant of Love

Readings: Joshua 24:1-2, 15-18; Ephesians 5:21-32; John 6:60-69

The gospel this Sunday concludes the Bread of Life discourse from the Gospel of John. The theme of covenant is added to the network of concepts that have developed from reflection on the Bread of Life.

The Book of Joshua describes the time in which the Israelites, who have been delivered from slavery in Egypt and sustained in the desert by God, take possession of God's gift of the Promised Land. The people are a new generation. The exodus generation died in the desert. There are also other people who did not come out of Egypt, some who joined the Israelites in the desert, some who became part of the community in the new land. All of the people need to renew their covenant commitment to God.

Joshua gathers the people in the center of the land at Shechem and recites the history of God's great deeds for them. He then presents them with a choice: Either serve the Lord who brought us out of Egypt or serve the other gods of the surrounding people. The people choose the service of the Lord. Joshua warns them that this choice will be difficult, but they stand firm.

The disciples of Jesus are also faced with a choice. This choice too is a covenant choice. Just as the Sinai covenant with God was sealed with a meal and a blood rite, both symbolizing shared life, so this covenant is sealed and renewed with a meal and in blood. The choice, however, is difficult. Many of the disciples cannot choose to remain with Jesus. Jesus reminds the disciples that the ability to make the covenant choice, the wise choice, is a gift from God. Peter, representing the Twelve, affirms their decision to stay with Jesus. They will share in the life-giving banquet of his words and his flesh. They will accept the gift of the covenant.

The reading from the Letter to the Ephesians is a section of a longer passage describing the mutual respect which should prevail in ordinary human relationships because of the new life shared in Christ. The relationship of marriage is particularly significant because the marriage relationship stands as a symbol of the covenant relationship between the people and God. The fidelity and love between husband and wife show us the fidelity and love between God and the people, between Christ and his Church. This is the new life of the covenant, chosen, renewed, and sustained at the banquet of the Eucharist.

Irene Nowell, OSB

Questions for Discussion

1. Why do you think sharing the Eucharist is the focus of many small and large gatherings of Christians (e.g., at a wedding, a family reunion, a parish anniversary, a Catholic teachers' conference, a CYO sports banquet)?

2. How is the bond celebrated at Eucharist like the bond celebrated in marriage? How do marriage partners strengthen their bond when they celebrate Eucharist together?

3. How does sharing the Body and Blood of Jesus bring you closer to your neighbors?

For Journaling

1. I find it difficult to believe when . . .

2. When I celebrate Eucharist with my family, I . . .

3. When I have a conflict with someone in the community of faith, I . . .

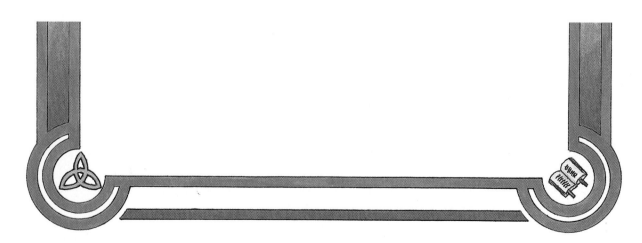

The Spirit of the Law

Readings: Deuteronomy 4:1-2, 6-8; James 1:17-18, 21-22, 27; Mark 7:1-8, 14-15, 21-23

All of us, at some time or another, have had the experience of trying to impress upon a small child the importance of obeying something we have asked them to do. It may be a matter of crossing a street, of safety around farm equipment or other machinery, of carefulness near a kitchen stove. We know that life can be harmed or destroyed in seconds, and we want to do everything within our power to insure that child's well-being. It's almost as if we cannot impress on that child enough the urgency and the importance of the words which we speak, for that child is precious in our eyes and loved greatly.

As the child gets older and more independent in his or her thinking, our "commands" can result in what at times seems like a tug-of-war. How do we get them to see that what we ask of them is not necessarily rooted in our own quest for power, or in the desire to deny their rights or their wishes for no reason other than that? How do we convince them that our "laws" stem from our desire to protect them from danger and to lead them in a way of happiness and well-being? They are precious in our lives and we love them.

These same sentiments underlay the biblical understanding of law. We are precious in God's eyes and God loves us. Accordingly, God gives us commandments to insure human happiness and well-being, and to lead us in the way of life that God has designed for us.

Today's first reading from Deuteronomy makes this very clear: "Hear the decrees which I am teaching you to observe that you may live." In other words, through keeping God's commandments, there is life, a life of peace, a life of happiness, a life close to God. This point is emphasized throughout the Book of Deuteronomy, a book whose compilation is placed at the time of the Babylonian exile.

In this time of separation from homeland (i.e., the Promised Land), in the aftermath of the destruction of the holy temple in Jerusalem, it surely must have seemed to Israel that its life as a nation was over and its uniqueness as the covenanted people of God without meaning. For the authors of Deuteronomy, Israel's tragic life-situation was its own doing, a result of infidelity and disobedience. Accordingly, the solution to Israel's problem was conversion and obedience.

This is the call God gives to Israel in Deuteronomy through His prophet Moses. These are the words Moses speaks to the people before he dies and before they enter the Promised Land. These are the words the authors of Deuteronomy speak to a nation in exile. "Choose life, then, that you and your descendants may live, by loving the Lord . . ." (Deuteronomy 30:19-20). This will insure a long life in the land which God has promised.

There is a certain irony in today's reading. Think for a moment about the situation of Israel in exile, of the impact the destruction of the temple would have had, the devastation and the hopelessness that would be felt. In the face of this, the authors of Deuteronomy can still call Israel "a great nation" (verse 6). In fact, it is not so much the authors of Deuteronomy who call Israel great, but the nations who see Israel settled on the land (and who will see that land resettled). Deuteronomy makes it clear, however, that Israel's greatness lies not in its own strength, but in God, who is close to it. Israel stays close to God when it is faithful, when it is obedient.

Exactly what this obedience consists of is the problem of today's gospel. The Pharisees were a group within Judaism who emphasized their exact observance of the law. The name *Pharisee* means "set apart," and indeed the Pharisees saw themselves as "set apart" from the rest of the people because of this outstanding faithfulness. The Pharisees tried to be faithful to the commandments written in Scripture (some 613 of them), as well as those which were given in their oral traditions. They were especially concerned with food laws and purity laws, because these were what distinguished Israel from the Gentile nations and marked Israel's uniqueness in God's eyes. It is these purification laws that are the issue in today's gospel.

Jesus does not deny the importance of these laws, but he does point out that some of the things to which some Pharisees cling so tenaciously are human traditions (and therefore can be changed), and not the law of God.

97

Furthermore, some of the Pharisees have neglected the more serious matters of the Law in terms of love of neighbor—a command Jesus makes explicit later in Mark's Gospel (12:29-31). This commandment, and love of God, summarizes all the others.

In not loving our neighbor—and Jesus spells out the ways that we don't—we are unfaithful. In not loving our neighbor, we are rendered "impure"—that is, defiled, tainted, not appropriate for that which is sacred and set apart for God.

The second reading, from the Letter of James, encourages us to welcome the word which has been planted in us. We might think of this word in terms of the Word who is Jesus, the word of the gospel, the word of all of Scripture. In our worship, in our prayer, in our reading of Scripture, the Holy Spirit "plants" the seed of God's grace. "Act on this," we are urged. For God wills to bring us to a new birth, a new life, God's new creation in Jesus—the "first-fruit," according to James. (For the Israelites, both the first-fruits of the crops and the firstborn of the flocks were sacrificed, set apart for God.)

As with Mark, James sees the evidence of this new life (or lack of it) in terms of our dealings with others. This is likewise the criterion for our "purity" (or suitability), for being "set apart" or consecrated to God.

Undoubtedly, there is a bit of the "Pharisee" in all of us. Like some of the Pharisees, we sometimes overlook the weightier matters of the Law in considering ourselves justified on the basis of our attention to more minor aspects of the law. On the other hand, perhaps we are inclined to rebel in the face of a command that is inconvenient or too difficult. Maybe we just haven't realized what is the basis of what God asks of us. It is nothing less than life.

Today's readings invite us to consider our stance. "Choose life," exhorts Deuteronomy. Life is chosen, says James, in hearing the word and acting on it. It is by the fruit of our works that we are known and judged. At the same time, the readings remind us that we are not left alone. It is God who has called us and initiated a covenant with us. It is God who graces us and desires to lead us into new and fuller life. It is God who stands before us and says, "You are precious in my eyes and I love you. Do this, and you shall live."

Anne Marie Sweet, OSB

Questions for Discussion

1. When you need to make an important decision, what steps do you take to discern what direction to take? What helps you to get to the "heart of the matter"?

2. How would you explain to an unbeliever what is essential to living a good Christian life?

3. What is more important, understanding the letter of the law or obeying the letter of the law? Explain your answer.

For Journaling

1. I neglect the more important parts of life when I . . .

2. Keeping the law is . . .

Open to God

Readings: **Isaiah 35:4-7; James 2:1-5; Mark 7:31-37**

It is not at all uncommon anymore to turn on the TV and find that the evening news or a favorite program has been "closed-captioned for the hearing impaired." Similarly, an elevator control panel in any public building is now marked with both Arabic and Braille numerals. These are but a few of the efforts undertaken in recent years to open up previously inaccessible parts of our world to those with physical impairments. These have been important steps.

Today's Scriptures likewise have to do with physical impairments and the freeing of that which was bound, the opening of new possibilities and new life. In this case, though, the results far exceed that which can be accomplished by mere human efforts. Today we are reminded that true healing, wholeness, and the restoration of human community are accomplished through the power of God and of Jesus, His Anointed One.

In the mind of the Israelites and their first-century descendants, illness and infirmity were punishments from God. (Recall, for example, the question of Jesus' disciples in John 9:2 regarding the man who was blind from birth: "Rabbi, was it his sin or that of his parents that caused him to be born blind?") As a result, people with infirmities were often shunned. Not only did they suffer from their physical impairments, they also were subjected to being treated as somehow inferior!

Sometimes, the biblical writers speak of deafness and blindness in a figurative sense, that is, as spiritual deafness or blindness (cf. Isaiah 42:18-19). The people are unable to hear the words that God speaks or to see the wonders that God performs.

It is difficult to know in what sense the prophet Isaiah is speaking of the deaf and the blind. The historical context of this chapter is unclear. Its language is similar to chapters 40-66. These chapters, often referred to as Deutero- or Second Isaiah, were written after the exile and speak words of comfort and encouragement to Israel through the promise of deliverance and restoration. Perhaps Isaiah is deliberately ambiguous about deafness and blindness in today's reading and wants his readers to consider both the literal and figurative dimensions.

Today's reading looks forward to a coming age of glory when all Israel's "infirmities" will be removed. This will be the age of the messiah, God's anointed one, who comes to bring salvation to Israel. It will be a time when Israel is no longer oppressed by its enemies and when the power of evil will no longer be manifest in sickness or afflictions of any kind.

Isaiah's words today speak to those who are fearful in the face of their sufferings as they await the Lord's deliverance. They are called to be strong, not to be afraid, for God is faithful and God will rescue them. On this day of salvation, all creation will be touched as afflictions of every kind will be wiped out. It will indeed be a time of a new creation.

These signs of the new creation, of the messianic age, are recalled by Jesus in the Gospel of Luke when the disciples of John the Baptist come to him and ask if he is the messiah. Jesus tells them to go and tell John what they see and hear: "The blind recover their sight, cripples walk, lepers are cured, the deaf hear, the dead are raised to life, and the poor have the good news preached to them" (Luke 7:22).

In today's gospel from Mark, we hear the story of one such incident. Jesus is ministering in Galilee. This geographical detail is important, for Galilee was Gentile territory. The Jews looked down upon the Gentiles, for they did not belong to the covenanted people. The Gentiles (non-Jews) were considered unclean because they did not abide by the laws (purity, food, circumcision) which marked Israel as sacred to God. The deaf man with the speech impediment in today's gospel not only had his physical afflictions against him—he was a Gentile.

It is interesting to think for a moment about the people who bring this Gentile deaf man to Jesus. We can assume that they too are Gentiles. What great faith in Jesus they must have had, what belief in his power to heal! Mark describes Jesus' healing activity in terms very similar to those used by other writers of his day (Jewish and Greek) in describing miracles, strange though they may seem to us. Nevertheless, it is striking that the man is healed when Jesus "touches" the parts of him that are weak and impaired.

The people are amazed at what Jesus has done. They spread the news throughout the cities, in spite of Jesus' admonition that they remain quiet about it. This exhortation to silence is a characteristic of Mark's Gospel. Scholars refer to it as Mark's "messianic secret," because Mark doesn't openly reveal Jesus' identity in his Gospel until the very end (15:39). Even then, it is a Gentile, a centurion, who recognizes just who Jesus is (as it is the Gentiles who recognize his power in today's gospel).

One other significant point on today's gospel: the Greek word which refers to the man's speech impediment is the same word used in the Greek translation of the Hebrew Scriptures (the Septuagint) in Isaiah 35:5, today's first reading. Mark would have used this translation and may therefore be making a definite connection with this reading from Isaiah.

The reading from James may at first seem quite unrelated to the first reading and the gospel. Nevertheless, it shares a common focus—affliction and oppression. In this case, the affliction is economic. And, as with all the others—Gentiles, the blind, the deaf, the person with a speech impairment—the poor are shunned.

James challenges us to look and see if we are those "others." The impairments, the poverty, may take many forms. James' position is very clear with regard to discrimination, and his position is very much rooted in the gospel tradition. One thing today's readings make quite clear: God has a special concern for the poor and the needy, and God acts on their behalf. If we are to be godlike, and that is our call, we must share this concern both in thought and in deed.

Today's Scriptures challenge us to look at our prejudices and instructs us to let them go. Today's Scriptures invite us to share in God's salvific activity by working to free people from the shackles of oppression, whatever form it may take. Today's Scriptures reach to the deaf, the blind, and the impaired parts of ourselves. The word is, "Be opened! . . . Be healed!" In Jesus, a new age has dawned. There is no need to fear. Our God has come to save us.

Anne Marie Sweet, OSB

Questions for Discussion

1. A father who loses his son in a racially motivated killing now vows, "I have finally come to know my mission in life; I shall not rest until I see justice done. I will do all I can, with every fiber of my being, to assure that justice rules in this land." What do you think he means by justice? How does that understanding compare with the teaching in today's readings?

2. Have you ever worked with or cared for a handicapped child or adult? What insights did you gain from that experience? Are there ways we shun people who are handicapped? What can be done to free them?

3. All of us are handicapped in some way. What hope do today's readings offer us?

For Journaling

1. My greatest handicap is . . .

2. The gift I have received from people with physical or mental handicaps is . . .

3. I grow in understanding God's ways when . . .

Twenty-Fourth
Sunday in Ordinary
Time

Faith in Action

Readings: **Isaiah 50:5-9; James 2:14-18; Mark 8:27-35**

When I was a child, it seemed that one of my mother's favorite expressions was "Actions speak louder than words." Needless to say, I hated it, probably because whenever she said it I knew that my actions weren't in line with my words. Nevertheless, there is a lot of truth in my mother's little saying.

This is the truth which is at the heart of today's Scripture readings. Actions—especially actions rooted in faith—speak louder than words or faith alone. Just as words without actions are insufficient, so is faith without actions. This is the message which is found in each one of our readings today.

The first reading, from the prophet Isaiah, is from one of the passages which is referred to as a Suffering Servant song. There are four such passages in Isaiah (Isaiah 42:1-9, 49:1-7, 50:4-9, 52:13-53:12). All of them speak of an individual (or of the community as a whole, as some scholars suggest, or both) who is chosen by God for a special mission on behalf of the people. This mission involves the "action" of suffering. In fact, it is through the servant's suffering that the mission is effective.

The servant is a person of faith. He is depicted as a person of prayer, whose ear is "opened" each morning by the word that God speaks. It is this word of God that the servant carries to those who are afflicted, in the hope that it will encourage them. In this role, the servant functions as a prophet, that is, as one who speaks God's word.

The servant does not turn his back when it becomes obvious that fidelity to his mission and to God's word will cost something. He willingly endures the suffering which comes his way because he knows that God is with him. He believes that God will deliver him.

These Songs of the Suffering Servant are found in the second part of the Book of Isaiah (Deutero-Isaiah), comprising chapters 40-66. These chapters stem from the period of Israel's exile in Babylon, a time of desolation, a time of alienation. Isaiah's words comfort the nation and remind them that they are God's people. God is faithful to the promises of old. God will not forsake them. They must be a people of faith, a living faith.

In the early days of the Church, these words of Isaiah reminded the Christians of Jesus and his suffering. Although this passage from Isaiah is not specifically quoted in today's gospel from Mark, there is a strong emphasis on the willingness to suffer (verse 34). We note also that Jesus, who has been teaching, is thought to be a prophet (verse 28).

The suggestion that he is a prophet is in response to his question asking the disciples what people thought about his identity. When he asks the disciples, his followers—literally, those who listened to his words—Peter answers, "You are the messiah." This recognition undoubtedly is an act of faith. However, Jesus is quick to spell out what his messiahship means—action, the action of suffering and death and resurrection.

This was too much for Peter. Unlike the servant in Isaiah, who heard the word which God spoke and did not rebel, Peter objects immediately. Jesus quickly sets him straight. This way of suffering, death, and resurrection was the way which God had ordained. As incomprehensible as this way might be, Jesus knew that in it, as in all things, God would be his help (Isaiah 50:7, 9).

This way, Jesus tells those who would hear him, must be the way of all who would come after him. It is not a passive way, as there are three active verbs in verse 35. A person must deny or renounce his or her own desires or wishes, his or her very self. A person must pick up and carry whatever cross or burden befalls him or her and must follow after Jesus. The paradox is that, in this suffering and death, there is resurrection. In this losing of self, one finds one's true self in God.

One way followers of Jesus are called to deny themselves is by actively responding to the needs of others. This is an important part of Jesus' teaching. See, for example, the story of the Last Judgment in Matthew 25:31-40. Whatever you do for another person, you do for me, is what Jesus says. Feeding the hungry, giving drink to the thirsty, welcoming the stranger, clothing the naked, taking care of the sick, visiting prisoners—these are the criteria by which we will be judged on the last day. These actions (or lack of them) are signs of our faithfulness in following Jesus. On another occasion Jesus said that all the commandments could be summed up in two: love of God and love of neighbor.

It is love in action—a decision, not a natural feeling—and it costs. The cost may be minimal at times, merely a slight inconvenience. Or it may be felt more intensely in a denial of self to meet the need of another. It may even cost one's life. But it proves one's following of Jesus.

These are the actions that James speaks of in today's second reading. Faith without works is dead. Such a faith does not lead to life. Needless to say, James is not trying to play down the importance of faith. In fact, the kinds of works that Jesus calls us to can only be done if they are rooted in faith. They call for a tremendous selflessness—this renouncing of self that is spoken of in today's gospel. They call for a great love, a love that is possible only if we walk in the way of Jesus, with the grace of the Lord God as our help.

Actions speak louder than words. What good are words without actions to give them credibility? What good is faith without practicing it? Only when our words are proven true by our actions, when our faith gives rise to works, do we truly follow the way of Jesus. In doing this, we know with the psalmist, in the response to today's first reading, that we walk in the way of God in the land of the living.

Anne Marie Sweet, OSB

Questions for Discussion

1. Our parish is a visible sign of the faith of our community. Do the activities of our parish speak of faith in Jesus? In what way?

2. In what ways are human standards different from God's standards? Which standards usually guide our decisions? Which standards would you like to have applied to you? Why?

3. Suffering makes some people bitter. Others become more compassionate to those in need. Why do you think this is true? What insights are offered by today's readings?

For Journaling

1. The most difficult part of my faith is . . .

2. When suffering comes my way, . . .

The Cross of Salvation

Readings: **Numbers 21:4-9; Philippians 2:6-11; John 3:13-17**

The cross is one of the most powerful and meaningful signs of our Christian identity. We are marked by the sign of the cross at our baptism. The Sign of the Cross is one of the first prayers parents teach their children. We hang a cross in our homes and display it atop our church buildings. The cross is often the center of focus in places where Christians gather.

This celebration of the Holy Cross brings us face to face with the irony of this Christian sign. The cross was, after all, an instrument of execution and a sign of shame. This instrument of execution has become the symbol of our salvation. The cross reminds us that Jesus, in being executed as a criminal, wins victory over death. An instrument of torture and death is the means of grace and salvation. It is at this moment of intense pain and suffering that God is most present.

So the cross becomes for us a symbol both of sin and salvation. It speaks the truth that Jesus has saved us. And it also proclaims that we too must carry our cross and die with him. But if we die with him we will also rise with him.

There are reminders of this powerful Christian symbol around us everywhere. They are present in the most mundane and ordinary items—the telephone pole, the fence post, the chair, the blind on our window, the stop sign, and the mail box. Each time we see the cross, we can rejoice in this sign of our salvation.

The Feast of the Holy Cross had its beginnings in the time of the Emperor Constantine. Constantine had mandated tolerance of Christianity, and Christians began to erect and dedicate public buildings. They also began publicly to display their treasured relics of the saints. In Jerusalem Christians began to publicly venerate the places where Christ had walked, especially on the way to Calvary. The Church there even discovered a cross which they believed to be the cross on which Christ had died. On September 13, 335, the Basilica of the Resurrection, built by Constantine in Jerusalem, was dedicated. On the next day the Church in Jerusalem held a solemn ceremony of veneration for the relic of the cross, which Cyril of Jerusalem is said to have discovered.

From that time on, the cross has been a public sign. As a public sign, it can be ambiguous. Like a flag, it can be used to legitimate causes that do not really reflect the values of Christ. The cross has served not only as a sign of peace and salvation, but also at times as a sign of division and even hatred. It has been used as the insignia on military shields, on badges of warriors, and as a sign of prejudice and persecution by groups like the Ku Klux Klan.

But the cross also has a cosmic significance. For many peoples, even those not acquainted with Christianity, the cross has been a sign that pulls together the four directions, all points, all elements, all peoples. For Christians, this cosmic significance is summed up in the cross of Christ. In Christ all peoples are gathered together into one. The cross witnesses to the depth of God's love for all people.

The sign of the cross endures as a sign to each of us of Christ's total gift of love. As we bless ourselves with the sign of the cross, we retrace the mark that was made upon us in our baptism. It is a sign that marks us as those won by Christ's death on the cross. Each time we see or make the sign, we deepen our awareness of who we are as Christians. We are also pointing beyond the present to the hope that is yet to be fulfilled in each of us in our death and final rising at the end of time.

In the readings for today's celebration, we see the mystery of the cross in striking contrast. In the first reading from the Book of Numbers, we see the people of Israel near the end of the journey to the Promised Land. They are complaining to Moses and to God about their unhappy plight. They are unhappy with the

103

food the Lord has provided, and they long to be back in Egypt. They have forgotten the pain and suffering they have left behind.

The story tells us that God punishes their ingratitude in the form of *saraph* (fiery) poisonous serpents. But God also provides a means for their healing. Moses is commanded to make an image of a fiery serpent and place it on a pole. All those who have been bitten need only look at the image to be saved from the deadly poison.

Whatever actually happened, the story has long served as a symbol of suffering and healing. The *caduceus,* used by pharmacists and physicians as a sign of healing, points out the fact that the medications we use are often "poisons" which, when taken in carefully prescribed ways, can lead to healing. The antidote for some snake bites is made from the venom of other snakes. The source of sickness becomes a source of healing. They are somehow the same reality. That which had been the cause of evil becomes the means for being saved. What is the cause of death become the means for life.

Jesus uses the story of the fiery serpents to suggest to Nicodemus the way of salvation. Nicodemus came to Jesus at night to find out more about what Jesus has been teaching. In a veiled way, Jesus' answer speaks of his future death on the cross. Just as the image of death in the serpent becomes the source of life, so too his own impending death will become the source of life.

Here John uses the term "lifted up," as he does throughout the Gospel, to mean both Jesus' being lifted up on the cross and his being lifted up by his resurrection and ascension. Just as the serpent became a source of life when it was lifted up, so will Jesus become a source of life when he is lifted up.

The celebration of the Feast of the Triumph of the Cross is a reminder that it is through the pain and suffering, the death and resurrection of Christ, that new life is won. Through Jesus we are brought to the fullness of life.

Jeanita F. Strathman Lapa

Questions for Discussion

1. In what way do the crosses we Christians display express our faith? In what way can crosses become a sign of division or even hatred?

2. What is the relationship between the cross and the problems of today's world? How can the cross liberate people? How has the cross been used to oppress people?

3. What are negative signs that became signs of salvation for you?

For Journaling

1. Whenever I see a cross, I . . .

2. The greatest cross in my life right now is . . .

3. The cross will lead to new life by . . .

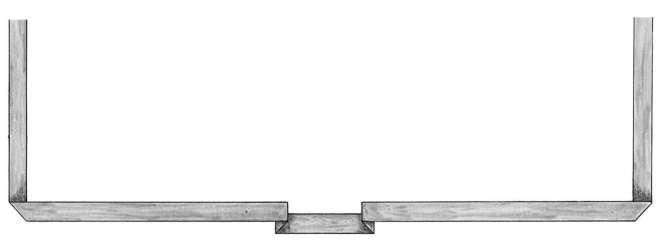

Twenty-Fifth Sunday
in Ordinary Time

Power and Powerlessness

Readings: **Wisdom 2:12, 17-20; James 3:16-4:3; Mark 9:30-37**

Some time ago, a television movie told the story of Jean Donovan, a twenty-six-year-old woman from Cleveland, Ohio. Impelled by the call of the gospel, she left her rather comfortable surroundings and joined a lay-volunteer organization of the Cleveland diocese. This young woman's missionary calling took her to the troubled country of El Salvador. She went, as part of a team, to proclaim the gospel of Christ. Proclaiming this gospel meant more than talking about the Lord who died and was raised to life. It meant ministering to the needs of the poor and oppressed people in countless ways.

For this young lay woman and three women religious with whom she worked, commitment to the gospel resulted in death. Like Jesus, these present-day martyrs were "put to death." Like the just person in today's first reading from the Book of Wisdom, they were tortured by those who found obnoxious their commitment to righteousness.

It is almost inconceivable that this martyrdom could happen in our day. It is almost unthinkable that anyone could give up so much, even if only temporarily, to live and work among the poor of another country. It is almost unimaginable that anyone would choose to go to a place where one's life was in danger—and to continue working there when one's work causes that danger. It doesn't make sense.

Neither did the teaching in today's gospel. This teaching abounds in paradoxes. First of all, there is the striking contrast between the images conjured up by the title *Son of Man* and the stark realities of being handed over and put to death. For the Jewish people of New Testament times, the title *Son of Man* brought to mind a savior figure. Although in its most literal meaning it refers to a human being, the reference to "one like a Son of Man," in Daniel 7:13, suggests that this human being receives an exalted status in heaven. He is a royal figure, served by many people and nations; his kingdom will last forever. This exalted one is in the presence of the Ancient of Days (God).

Yet, what Jesus says about the Son of Man in today's gospel is not glorious. It is not a picture of exaltation, but of humiliation, of torture. Of course, Jesus adds the part about rising after three days, but the disciples don't understand what any of it means.

There are three places in Mark's Gospel where Jesus "predicts" his passion. Biblical scholars suggest that, while Jesus may indeed have recognized that his death was imminent due to the rising tide of opposition, the precise wording of the events as given here in Mark 9:31 probably reflects Mark's interpretation after the fact. Mark's Gospel was written around A.D. 70, almost forty years after the death of Jesus. Mark's purpose was not to give an historical account comparable to our television on-the-scene reporting, but to interpret the meaning which the events of Jesus' life had for the community of his time—the contemporary disciples of Jesus.

Equally as paradoxical as a humiliated Son of Man is the idea of greatness being found in servanthood. The word used here for "servant" is also used for "a waiter at table." Undoubtedly, what the twelve had in mind was being seated in the places of honor at the table!

The paradoxes continue in the saying about welcoming a child. In the culture of Jesus' day, a child had no rights. Like a slave, the child was almost considered a possession. In this saying, Jesus tells the Twelve to welcome or receive a child. The Twelve would never advance in status by welcoming a child. A child had no power or prestige; a child was lowly and helpless. In welcoming those with no rights, no power, no prestige, the disciples were, in fact, welcoming Jesus. What is more, God the Father, who sent Jesus, is welcomed. Mark's message is powerful: God is met in the powerless, those who are without rights of their own.

Even more, not only is God met in the person of the lowly one, God has a special interest in the cause of the lowly one. God exalts those who are lowly (literally "humble"), says Mary, while those who are mighty are deposed (Luke 1:52). This theme is found repeatedly throughout Scripture.

Today's first reading casts somewhat of a different light on this theme, for it is not so much a case of the lowly being exalted as it is of the just one being persecuted or humiliated by the wicked. Life does not seem to improve for the one who tries to live faithful to God's law. Quite the contrary, it appears to worsen.

"Justice" and "humility" are two important biblical themes. While a full discussion of these two themes would call for much more attention than we can give here, let us briefly define them as follows: a person is "just" if he or she tries to live in the right relationship with God and with other people, that is, in accord with righteousness as defined by God's law. The "humble" person is aware that he or she is a creature of God, a steward of God's gifts, and accountable to the Creator. Like the just person, the humble person strives to live in accord with God's law.

Often a great amount of trust is called for from those who are just and humble. The troubles and afflictions of their lives seem anything but blessed. These people are called to strong faith. Indeed, the situations of their lives can deepen their faith (or turn them to despair, as in the case of the disciples before they experienced the risen Jesus). For those who try to live justly and humbly, life is at times lived in the darkness of the three days between death and resurrection.

Today's first reading tells us nothing of the reaction of the just one. The focus is on the thoughts of the wicked. The second reading for today is concerned with the source of the wickedness that is demonstrated here. James is very clear about the origins of wickedness, particularly in the two verses preceding the section chosen for today's reading. The behavior described is not in accord with the heavenly ways of God's righteousness, and is even termed diabolical. James goes on to describe the conduct proper to those who try to live in accord with God's ways. Although the context of James' words indicates that he is addressing Christian teachers, his remarks on conduct are surely applicable to all.

Today's readings speak to us of several themes important for our Christian lives. First of all, we are confronted with the reality of suffering, the suffering of Jesus as well as our own. We are reminded that sometimes our Christian commitment calls us to live in the darkness of the time between death and resurrection, between the pain of persecution and the strength of our hope that God will take care of us.

There is a call to examine ourselves as well. God forbid that we be the ones who persecute another, who oppress, who in any way kill the life of another. The way of Jesus is clearly set out for us. We must welcome the lowly. We must indeed become lowly ourselves, seeking not importance but servanthood. We must not only endure suffering, we must receive it, absorb it, and allow God to transform it into new life.

The attempt of Jean Donovan to do this has been vividly portrayed in a drawing by a woman artist from the Midwest. The drawing is a crucifixion scene, and on each arm of the cross there hangs the body of one of the four women killed in El Salvador. Because of our faith in the risen Jesus, we can say with them, "The Lord upholds my life."

For the story of Jean Donovan, see the book, *Salvador Witness: The Life and Calling of Jean Donovan,* by Ana Carrigan (New York: Simon and Schuster, 1984).

Anne Marie Sweet, OSB

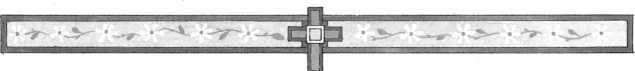

Questions for Discussion

1. Why does Jesus use the example of a small child to teach the disciples what it means to be great?

2. Many times those who are chronologically older or in a higher social status than others assume the right to tell younger people or those of lower social status what to do. Why do you think this happens? What would Jesus have us do?

3. What does power mean to you?

For Journaling

1. I feel powerful when . . .

2. I feel powerless when . . .

3. I am powerful when . . .

4. I am powerless when . . .

Twenty-Sixth Sunday
in Ordinary Time

Ecumenism

Readings: Numbers 11:25-29; James 5:1-6; Mark 9:38-43, 45, 47-48

Sad to say, there are probably few of us whose families have managed to escape disagreements over wills and inheritances. What is worse, these disagreements have caused alienation and bitterness, creating wounds which have festered for years. People tend to be jealously protective of what is seen to be rightfully and exclusively theirs. The gift becomes more important than the giver.

While today's readings are not concerned with wills, they are concerned with inheritances and bestowals. In both the first reading and the gospel, the gift which is given becomes a possession which is jealously guarded—so much so, in fact, that the leaders of God's people lose sight of the freedom and design of the God who bestows the gifts.

The first reading from Numbers is concerned with the men who assisted Moses in the leadership of the people. The term *elder* refers not necessarily to advanced age. Here it is used in a technical sense with reference to a person having authority. The seventy elders have authority because God's spirit has been bestowed on them. The seventy elders are prophets; they speak in God's name. They speak in God's name because they have God's spirit.

In the Hebrew Scriptures, authority was passed on or shared from one leader to another, usually by some sort of sign or ritual action. (See, for example, the story of Elijah and Elisha in 2 Kings 2.) In today's reading, two men are enabled to prophesy who were not present in the "official" gathering for the "bestowal" of authority (verse 16). The bulk of today's reading focuses on the reaction of Joshua, Moses' assistant, to this event. (Joshua succeeded Moses and led the people into the Promised Land. Those events are recorded in the Book of Joshua.)

The loyal Joshua could be seen as springing to Moses' defense. Eldad and Medad had not been authorized to prophesy, at least not from Joshua's perspective. While Joshua's intentions may have been good, Moses informs him that his loyalty is misplaced. The focus is not is to be on the earthly leader, but on God. Would that all the people might experience God's gifts!

A similar experience confronted the apostles in today's gospel. The apostles had been commissioned by Jesus to expel demons in Mark 6:7. The apostles were apparently successful in this activity (cf. Mark 6:30). Their dilemma arises when they see someone else who had not been in their group use this power. The expulsion of demons is a most important miraculous event in Mark. It signifies that Jesus has power over Satan. The people of New Testament times thought that certain illnesses (physical and mental) were caused by Satan. Accordingly, people with healing powers were perceived as miracle workers. The literature from this era indicates that there were a number of such miracle workers in Jesus' day.

What is significant in today's gospel is that the nonapostle exorcist performs his work in Jesus' name, that is, recognizing Jesus' power. The apostles are concerned that he is not of their group. Jesus is concerned about the bigger picture, the in-breaking of the kingdom of God.

One who works in the name of Jesus shares this concern. The "name of Jesus" gets repeated emphasis in the next verse even though it may not be apparent in the English translation. Literally, verse 41 reads, "for anyone who gives you a drink of water in [the] name [of Jesus] because you are of Christ. . . ." The emphasis is on recognizing and honoring the name of Jesus. Anyone who recognizes Jesus' name, whether or not the person belongs to the community, will be rewarded because the person honors Jesus' name.

Today we might ask ourselves if there is any of the Joshua, any of the John in us. Are we resentful of the faithful work of other Christians or of the Jews, our ancestors in faith? Are we able to esteem the commitment of the non-Christian members of our human family? Or is such a step too much of an obstacle for us, as it was, at least initially, for Joshua and John?

The latter part of today's gospel is concerned with obstacles (literally, scandals) to discipleship. The disciples are warned about being an obstacle to other believers (*little ones*, perhaps a reference to people without power or significance in the community). It would be better to suffer a tortuous death than to give scandal to others.

If the cause of the obstacle stems from yourself, get rid of it! Jesus' highly figurative language clearly emphasizes that nothing is worth the fires of hell or Gehenna. (The name actually refers to Hinnon, a place south of Jerusalem, once the site of human sacrifice to a Canaanite god. In biblical tradition, Gehenna came to be associated with punishment and destruction by fire.) Better to suffer earthly loss than eternal punishment.

The letter from James chides Christians for their excessive concern for earthly riches. These have become an obstacle to their faith! Not only are they inordinately possessive of what they have accumulated, they have grown rich unjustly—at the expense of others! They are destined for destruction. Again, we might ask ourselves where we stand in this regard. What is our attitude toward our possessions—no matter what they are worth? Do we own them, look on them as things to use? Or do they own us? Are they really an obstacle for us? Do we have treasure in heaven—a treasure built up through faith and acts of justice? Or are we an obstacle, a scandal to others?

The note of joy in the verse which is today's responsorial psalm is a startling contrast to the admonitions of today's readings. Perhaps, as a result, it will gain our attention. "The precepts of the Lord give joy to the heart." We've heard the precepts of the Lord in today's readings. Only these can lead us to eternal life, to heavenly treasures. We pray this day, with the psalmist, that we might be diligent in keeping those precepts.

Anne Marie Sweet, OSB

Questions for Discussion

1. Are there obstacles to cooperation between Christians in our town? What causes these obstacles? What positive experiences of cooperation between Christians have you had?

2. Our own faith can be enriched by sharing with persons of another religion. Do you know anything about the teachings of other religions? How have they enriched your faith?

3. Why do differences often lead to separation and mistrust? How can we recognize those who teach in Jesus' name? In God's name?

For Journaling

1. A person outside of our Church who does God's work is . . .

2. I have been enriched by the faith of people of other religions when . . .

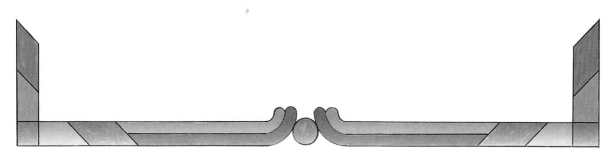

Marriage

Readings: Genesis 2:18-24; Hebrews 2:9-11; Mark 10:2-16

The Gospel of Mark, which has been read throughout this year, is moving steadily toward the final crisis of Jesus' life: his crucifixion and death. The confrontations with some of the Pharisees increase in frequency and tension.

In this Sunday's gospel some Pharisees attempt to trap Jesus in a very sticky question: the lawfulness of divorce. The Book of Deuteronomy made provision for protecting the woman involved in a divorce situation by demanding certain formal procedures. The fact of divorce is simply presumed there, but this passage was later interpreted as permission for divorce. Jesus turns the question from technicalities about the law to the heart of the matter: the true nature of marriage. He compares the passage in Deuteronomy, which is simply a concession to human weakness, to the creation story in Genesis, which is a description of human nature at its best.

The creation story in Genesis 2 centers on human beings. Reasons are given for their responsibility for the earth, the value of their work, and the goodness of sexuality and marriage. In the story which leads to the distinction between man and woman, male and female, the phrase "not good" is used for the first time in the creation accounts. Throughout Genesis 1 God looked at creation and found it "very good." Now it is pointed out that it is "not good" for the human creature (*'adam*) to be alone. He cannot yet be named "man" (*'ish*) because there is not yet a woman (*'ishshah*) as his equal partner. Not until verse 23 will both man and woman be named.

The story portrays God searching for an equal partner for the human being. The animals are not satisfactory; they are inferior. Only a creature which shares the same flesh will be a fitting partner. Because they share one flesh, it is in the very nature of their creation that they long to be reunited. That bond of union, coming from their very creation, is so central to human nature that, once it is realized, it cannot be dissolved. Marriage, the union of man and woman in one flesh, which is the way they were created to be, is forever.

This passage from Genesis is quoted by Jesus in answer to these Pharisees. He continues by suggesting several problems with their current practice. By divorcing their wives they are setting up the situation in which either party may seek another partner to marry. Jesus condemns this as adultery. Jesus' words also suggest the inequality of the divorce procedure. In Jewish practice only a man could divorce his wife; a woman could not divorce her husband. On the other hand, the woman was frequently the only party accused of adultery (see John 8:1-11). Jesus seems to assume that, if divorce were allowed, either party could divorce the other. He also presumes that both parties are responsible for the marriage bond and either could be accused of adultery. Jesus presumes equality in the marriage relationship.

The final passage in the gospel shows us Jesus welcoming and blessing children. There is a natural sequence between the discussion of marriage and the welcoming of children. Besides welcoming and blessing them, Jesus proclaims further that the kingdom belongs to those who receive it as children. In Jesus' time children were not regarded with the same tenderness and indulgence with which they often are today. The Book of Proverbs suggests that discipline for children was strict and often harsh. Jesus' statement in the gospel, therefore, does not suggest a romantic glorification of childhood. Rather it declares that disciples must accept the kingdom as those who are dependent, even as servants. Their model is Jesus who was made lower than the angels, who accepted death for the sake of all, who was made perfect through suffering (Hebrews 2:9-11).

Irene Nowell, OSB

111

Questions for Discussion

1. How does the teaching about sexuality in the first reading ground Christian sexuality and marriage? What is the reason for the indissolubility of marriage?

2. When the relationship between the marriage partners is strained by changes, growth, or selfishness, what helps to strengthen the marriage covenant?

3. What do you think is the best preparation for two people who are planning to be married?

4. Today married couples face many different problems than did the people in the first century. What do you think Jesus would say to married couples today? How do you think he would address these important concerns today?

For Journaling

1. The person who knows me best . . .

2. God has given me the gift of love by . . .

3. The greatest gift I bring to our marriage is . . .

4. The greatest gift my partner brings to our marriage is . . .

Searching for God

Readings   **Wisdom 7:7-11; Hebrews 4:12-13; Mark 10:17-30**

What is the one thing in life for which you would sacrifice everything else? Today's readings claim that the only true value is found in God. Nothing else lasts. Nothing else will buy life.

The first reading shows us wisdom as the source of all good. The claims are put in the mouth of Solomon, wisdom's patron saint. Actually the Book of Wisdom was written about 50 B.C.E., about nine hundred years after Solomon. But the claim is in the long tradition of wisdom writers.

According to the tradition, wisdom is the way to a good life. Human experience has confirmed that the possession of wisdom leads to a full life—wealth, health, successful children, honor, long life. Solomon, the possessor of great wealth and power, is the example of a truly wise person. A story in 1 Kings 3:1-14 tells that Solomon, given a choice by God, asks for a listening heart. God, pleased with the request, grants Solomon wisdom and all other good things besides (see 1 Kings 5:9-14).

For most wisdom writers, the rewards of wisdom had to be granted before death. Only in the last century before Christ did a belief in life after death begin to grow. Some faithful Jews began to see the reward of a full life as participation in God's kingdom after death as well as before. The demand to seek wisdom above all else, however, remained.

In today's gospel from Mark, Jesus meets a rich man who wishes to share in everlasting life. Jesus begins by checking the primary qualification: observance of the commandments. Assured on that point, Jesus presents the radical demand of the kingdom: Be prepared to abandon everything for the sake of following Jesus. The man leaves sadly. His trust in possessions prevent him from acquiring the riches of God's kingdom. Jesus does not soften the demand. Great possessions inspire great trust in material things. For those who are rich, in whatever way, it is harder to believe that the future kingdom could be worth more than present possessions.

The demand to choose the kingdom above all else is a major theme in Mark. The evangelist believed that the second coming of Christ was right around the corner. There was no time for indecision; the choice was urgent. Nothing should be allowed to stand in the way of a free, wholehearted commitment to the kingdom.

The ability to let go of everything for the sake of God's kingdom, however, is impossible for human beings. Human strength is not enough. Only God can give the vision to see the truly wise choice. Only God can give the power to make the choice. True life comes only from God.

Irene Nowell, OSB

Questions for Discussion

1. What is a "listening heart"? How does a "listening heart" make a person wise?

2. Possessions can get in the way of our following Jesus. What temptations do possessions offer?

3. A Christian bookstore was selling a wallet imprinted with the words, "Who is in charge?" Is the way we spend our money a sign of faith or lack of it?

For Journaling

1. What possessions are most difficult for me to surrender? Why?

2. What keeps me from giving myself completely to God is . . .

3. When Jesus calls me to follow him, I . . .

Christians Serve

Readings: **Isaiah 53:10-11; Hebrews 4:14-16; Mark 10:35-45**

Why do bad things happen to good people? This question, the title of a popular book, has bothered believers throughout history. Suffering was an even greater problem throughout most of Old Testament times when there was little or no belief in life after death. What does suffering mean? Why does it come to the wrong people, at the wrong time? How can suffering be part of a world created by a just God?

The passage from Isaiah is part of the section (chapters 40-55) written by an anonymous prophet just as the Babylonian exile was ending (around 587 B.C.E.). There are four songs in this section which describe the suffering of a servant of the Lord (Isaiah 42:1-4, 49:1-7, 50:4-11, 52:13-53:12). The servant is a mysterious figure. Sometimes he appears to be Israel in exile, or a prophet, or even Moses leading the new exodus. In each song the suffering of the servant increases. In this last song, as he is brought to the point of death, his suffering is revealed as atonement for the guilt of others. Because of his willingness to endure suffering for the sake of others, the servant is saved from death and granted a long life.

The New Testament authors were faced with a critical problem concerning the suffering of Jesus. Nowhere in Jewish expectation was suffering linked with the figure of the messiah. One solution to the question of a suffering messiah was the linking of the figure of the messiah with the figure of the suffering servant. Thus Christians, reading the Servant Songs now, think immediately of the passion of Jesus, whose suffering was a ransom for our sins.

The Gospel of Mark, which we have been reading throughout this year, illustrates the problem of a suffering messiah by continually pointing out the misunderstanding by the disciples, especially of Jesus' mission.

Today's gospel follows Jesus' third prediction of his passion. The response of the disciples to each prediction has been misunderstanding (see Mark 8:31-33, 9:30-32). A month ago, on the Twenty-Fifth Sunday, the gospel reading told a story of the disciples' desire for prestige, part of their misunderstanding following the second passion prediction.

In this Sunday's story, two of the leaders among the disciples act out their misunderstanding of Jesus' mission. James and John are looking for glory. Jesus tells them that he can guarantee them only a share in his suffering. They ask for positions of honor in the kingdom. Jesus tells them that the only position they should seek is the position he has assumed, that of a servant. In the end, as they follow him, they too will be called to give their lives.

Even as the Gospel of Mark places terrific demands on Jesus' followers, the Letter to the Hebrews gives them courage. Jesus, who has gone before us, knows our weakness, has shared our suffering, and has won the victory for all of us. Therefore, we may approach Jesus without fear, and he will give us mercy, favor, and help.

The mystery of suffering is not removed by these readings. Rather, the mystery is heightened. Not only is suffering still a part of human life, but even God in Jesus has willed to share our human experience of suffering. And Jesus' suffering does not remove our pain, even though his suffering for us and his victory over sin and death for our sake does give meaning to a human experience which otherwise seems to be meaningless. His sharing in our suffering and his victory over pain and death are our pledge of a share in his risen glory.

Irene Nowell, OSB

Questions for Discussion

1. Why was the idea of a "suffering messiah" so hard for the disciples to accept?

2. Some people refuse to believe in a loving God because they see so much suffering in the world. Does this argument seem reasonable to you? Does it challenge your faith?

3. How can suffering heal divisions and bring people together? Have you ever had this experience?

For Journaling

1. Because God has shared in our human experience of suffering, I . . .

2. When I see people who suffer, I . . .

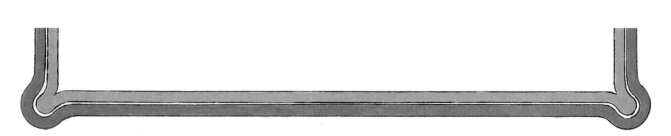

Power in Weakness

Readings: **Jeremiah 31:7-9; Hebrews 5:1-6; Mark 10:46-52**

Sometimes we have the idea that following Jesus, being faithful disciples, is something we accomplish on our own. Today's readings should cure us of that mistaken idea once and for all. Our faith is a gift of God; our discipleship is through the power of God.

The prophet Jeremiah preached just as Judah was being taken into exile in Babylon (587 B.C.E.). The northern kingdom, Israel, had been exiled by Assyria over a century earlier (722 B.C.E.). The consoling passages at the end of the Book of Jeremiah were probably addressed originally to the already captive northern kingdom (sometimes called Jacob or Ephraim). Later Jeremiah's words were adapted to comfort Judah and give hope that the Babylonian exile would end soon. Thus today's passage sounds very much like the second section of the Book of Isaiah (chapters 40-55), which was written just as the Babylonian exile was ending.

The prophet proclaims God's intention to bring a remnant of the people back from Babylon, the land of the north. The remnant will be a faithful people, in contrast to the rebellious people who were punished with exile. The remnant will be made up of those who have no strength of their own except in God—the lame, the blind, pregnant women, and those in labor. These are the most vulnerable people in any traveling group. These are precisely the people God will bring back on this triumphant journey. For these frail ones God will provide water in the desert and a smooth road (cf. Isaiah 35:1-10, 40:3-5). These people, who know that their only hope is God, will return with joyful shouting.

Jeremiah 31 is full of signals that God brings the people back home because of God's own fidelity to the covenant. God renews the wedding promise: I will be their God; they will be my people (31:1). God renews the promise of covenant love (*hesed,* 31:3). God recommits Himself to the parent/child relationship of the covenant (31:9; cf. Exodus 4:22). Finally God promises a new covenant (31:31-34). The remnant who return will be the new covenant people.

For the last several Sundays, the Gospel of Mark has been showing us how difficult it is for the disciples to understand Jesus' own mission and, therefore, to understand the implications of following him. Today's gospel forms the end of a section (8:22-10:52) in which the disciples are beginning to get a glimmer that Jesus is the Messiah, but they are still in the dark concerning the fact that he must suffer in order to enter into his glory (cf. 8:31-33, 9:31-32, 10:35-45).

Bookends around this section are two stories about the cure of a blind man (8:22-26, 10:46-52). Before the first cure, Jesus complains that the disciples have eyes, but do not see (8:18). The first blind man is cured only in stages (8:25). The second blind man is cured "immediately" (10:52). The second blind man also calls Jesus by a messianic title, *Son of David.* He declares his desire to see, and as soon as he is cured he begins to follow Jesus, thus becoming a disciple. It is impossible not to see the two blind men as examples of what is happening to the disciples. They don't see. They call Jesus *messiah.* They struggle for faith. But, even in blindness, they continue to follow Jesus.

Faith is a gift; discipleship is through the power of Jesus. The Letter to the Hebrews tells us that even Jesus, the Son of God, did not take the office of high priest upon himself, but received it as a gift. Having received the gift, the Son of God is established exclusively as king (chapter 1) and high priest (5:5-6) by the Father. Yet he has compassion for us since he shares our human nature.

Irene Nowell, OSB

Questions for Discussion

1. God often works through those who are least important and weak in the eyes of the world. What examples can you give of this phenomenon?

2. What situations in our world today most need the power of God? Through whom does God work?

For Journaling

1. When I cannot see . . .

2. I need the power of God . . .

3. My weakness . . .

God's Friends

Readings: **Revelation 7:2-4, 9-14; 1 John 3:1-3; Matthew 5:1-12**

It is the beginning of November, and autumn harvesting is almost complete. We have packed away our summer things. Many homes and front yards have been decorated with fruits of the harvest. Pumpkins, squash, and corn decorate the fronts of many homes. This is the time of nature's resting after the harvest. It is a time of change. Trees and shrubbery display their beauty in new robes of reds and yellows, oranges and browns. Nature begins its time of dying so that life can be born anew in the splendor of springtime greenness.

The Church celebrates a harvest festival, too, a feast in honor of all saints followed by a day to remember the souls in purgatory. It is an appropriate time to celebrate the vision of God's harvest at the end of time. As the cycle of the seasons changes, it is also a time to look at the seasons of our lives. We look at our own lives to see what harvest is there. We are brought face to face with the dying and changing that is happening within ourselves. And we await in hope the springtime growth which our present dying will bring about.

The first reading for the Solemnity of All Saints is taken from the Book of Revelation. The Book of Revelation was written during a time when Christians were being persecuted for their faith. Today's selection gives us a vision of salvation as the final victory of those who are faithful. This final victory is described in highly symbolic language. The author portrays God's judgment that is about to fall on the earth. But he assures God's faithful servants that for them God's judgment will be deliverance.

The sign of the deliverance of the faithful will be a "seal on the forehead of the servants of God" (Revelation 7:3). This marking on the forehead echoes the account of the marking in the vision of Ezekiel 9:4, "Pass through the city . . . and mark an X on the foreheads of those who moan and groan over all the abominations that are practiced within it."

Most of us have seen enough western movies to be familiar with the practice of branding. Ranchers mark their cattle, horses, or sheep with the specific brand to show ownership. Cattle bearing a certain brand belong to the rancher whose mark this is, and they are under that rancher's protection and care. In the ancient world it was a widespread custom for lords to impress the seal of their ring on their belongings. Whatever bore this seal belonged to the lord and was, therefore, under his protection. The meaning of the sealing in today's reading becomes clear. Whoever bears "the seal of the living God" is under God's protection and will be given the strength necessary to persevere until the end. This word of encouragement from the writer to the believers who are suffering persecution is also a word of encouragement to each of us. We too have been sealed and named as God's and will be given the strength necessary to endure any hardship or suffering.

"Who are these people all dressed in white? And where have they come from?" (Revelation 7:13) That huge crowd which no one could count are all the saints. The reading from the First Letter of John helps us to identify the saints. Saints are God's sons and daughters. But they are saints, not so much because of what they have done, but because of the love of God which empowers them. John reminds us how much God loves each one of us by calling us His sons and daughters. The full meaning of God's love is still to be revealed to us, John says. Then, at that end time, we shall be like the risen Lord and we shall see God "as He is."

Today is a day to remember all those men and women who have lived faithfully in the past. But it is also a time to remember our own destiny. These readings challenge us to bring our own lives into focus and celebrate the possible saint within each of us. We are reminded of our own struggle to be whole, to be "pure of heart."

This brief powerful reminder is echoed in yet another way in the Gospel of Matthew. Matthew presents here a basic way of life for all Christians to follow. The call to live as sons and daughters of God is a call to change one's entire life, to abandon oneself totally to God. Here Jesus addresses especially all the "anawim," the "little people," the simple faith community. His words to his disciples and to each of us are a call to holiness, to completion by deep interior change of heart. It is a call to let go of all that keeps us from following the way of generosity, openness, and compassion. It is a call to be pure of heart, to be single-hearted, committed as whole persons to God and one's brothers and sisters. It is a call to be full of fruitfulness—to be ripe . . . to be ready for the harvest at the fullness of time—the day of the Lord.

The celebration of the feast of All Saints is followed by the feast of All Souls. We recognize that our conversion, our commitment to God and to His people might not be complete while we are in this life. And so Catholics have maintained a tradition of praying for their loved ones who have died, that their conversion, their purification, might be complete and they might rejoice with all the saints in heaven.

There is a wide selection of readings possible for the Feast of All Souls. Perhaps a useful meditation for us would be to choose a reading that speaks to us now of our faith in the resurrection of Jesus and of "our hope that our departed brothers and sisters will share in his resurrection."

Jeanita F. Strathman Lapa

Questions for Discussion

1. How does nature reflect the cycles of life and death, dying and rising, growth and change?

2. Why do you think it is difficult for many of us to see ourselves as saints? What qualities or characteristics mark saints?

3. What images of life after death are most attractive for you?

For Journaling

1. Whenever I think of myself as a saint, I . . .

2. The saint I most admire is . . .

Love of God and Love of Neighbor

Readings: **Deuteronomy 6:2-6; Hebrews 7:23-28; Mark 12:28-34**

What is the one essential thing for leading a good life? That is the question of Jesus' time, just as in today's gospel. In the Jewish tradition of Jesus' time, just as in today's Jewish and Christian traditions, there were many regulations and recommendations for piety. Fasting, prayer, works of charity, support of religious ministers, as well as many regulations for keeping the commandments, all were contained in the Jewish Law. The scribe in today's gospel seeks the heart of the matter.

The first reading contains the command that was and is seen to be central in Jewish tradition: "Hear, O Israel. The Lord is our God, the Lord alone! Therefore, you shall love the Lord your God with all your heart, and with all your soul, and with all your strength" (Deuteronomy 6:4-5). That command is central to Deuteronomy. Throughout the book the equation is drawn out: to fear the Lord equals to love the Lord equals to obey the Lord. Doing this will bring life to the people; disregarding this will bring exile and death.

The command "to love the Lord" is borrowed from ancient Near Eastern treaty forms. In the treaty, the inferior nation is commanded to love the king of the superior nation. In Deuteronomy Israel describes the covenant with God in the treaty form. But Israel's understanding of the covenant with God is far deeper than a treaty. Israel considers the relationship with God to be as powerful as the bond between husband and wife or between parent and child. Thus the command to love is the obvious demand of the relationship.

The passage in Deuteronomy continues with a set of instructions which indicate the importance of this command. These words are to be remembered day and night, at home and away, at work or at rest. They are to be drilled into the children, and reminders are to be put on the door. They are to be as close to the heart as one's wrist, as close to the mind as one's forehead.

In Jewish tradition these words have indeed been taken to heart. The believer recites the Shema (so called from the first word, *Shema*—hear) when getting up and going to bed. All Jewish prayer begins with the Shema. One of the oldest scraps of manuscript we have of the Hebrew Bible, the Nash Papyrus (first or second century B.C.E.), contains the Shema and the Ten Commandments.

Thus Jesus is certainly in tune with the progression of Jewish tradition when he answers the scribe's question. Jesus adds to this command from Deuteronomy a second command from Leviticus: "You shall love your neighbor as yourself" (Leviticus 19:18). Chapter 19 of Leviticus is a whole series of commands on various things under the heading: "Be holy, for I, the Lord, your God, am holy" (Leviticus 19:2). Covenant members are to be like God. God cares for others; they should, too.

The combination of these two commandments may be original with Jesus. The scribe adds yet another idea from the Hebrew Bible: Loving God is worth more than sacrifice. The prophet Samuel reminded Saul that "obedience (= love) is better than sacrifice" (1 Samuel 15:22; see Hosea 6:6). The scribe recognizes these two commandments as the heart of the matter, more important than worship.

The relationship between the scribe and Jesus is the most positive of Jesus with a scribe in all the Gospels. The scribe commends Jesus for the wisdom of his answer; Jesus commends the scribe for his insight. Their conversation is evidence that Jesus' rejection by the Jews was hardly total. It also demonstrates that Jesus' preaching was in line with some of the best Jewish belief of his day.

The reading from the Letter to the Hebrews discusses sacrifice and the priesthood necessary to perform it. In the first covenant there were many priests offering many sacrifices. This was necessary because priests who died needed to be replaced and the sacrifices offered were imperfect. But the sacrifice of Jesus, the divine sinless one, a sacrifice which was perfect love of God and neighbor, is the only sacrifice necessary in the new covenant. Jesus is appointed by the Father as permanent high priest (5:1–6). His sacrifice alone is necessary.

Irene Nowell, OSB

Questions for Discussion

1. What is most essential in our preaching and living of the gospel? How is this reflected in the way our parish lives?

2. How does our parish worship reflect what is most essential about being a Christian? Our parish budget? Our parish activities?

For Journaling

1. When I die, I would like people to be able to say . . .

2. What is most important to me . . .

We Are Called to Share

Readings: **1 Kings 17:10-16; Hebrews 9:24-28; Mark 12:38-44**

Widows hold center stage in this Sunday's readings. The widow in Israel was extremely vulnerable. She had no real means of economic independence. She was dependent either on her sons, her father's household, or society. For that reason there are many commands in the Law concerning care for widows. In today's readings we find widows exercising extreme generosity in turn. Neither of the two widows portrayed has anything to live on, yet each of them supports a religious leader or leaders.

As the story from 1 Kings begins, Elijah has just predicted a drought. The drought in the ninth century B.C.E. lasted three years and was extremely severe. It is also noted in the annals of one of the kings of Tyre. The brook near which Elijah lives has run dry, and so the Lord instructs him to go to Zarephath (about nine miles south of Sidon, outside Israelite territory).

The story of Elijah's meeting with the widow is typical of the stories in the Elijah/Elisha cycle. The editor has gathered several stories to illustrate the power of the prophetic word. A prophet speaks, and the word is fulfilled. Elijah promises the woman that, if she feeds him, neither she nor her son will starve. And that's the way it happens. The woman is an example of amazing faith. A non-Israelite, she believes the word of the Israelite prophet. She risks not only her life but that of her son. She feeds the prophet first, and God sustains her, the son, and the prophet for a year on her generosity.

Jesus also presents religious leaders demanding the savings of widows. The situation is somewhat different, however. Elijah demanded the last sustenance of the widow of Zarephath for survival. Through her faith and his word, both widow and prophet are sustained. Jesus portrays some scribes as demanding contributions from widows for their comfort and luxury. They are filled and the widows starve. In addition, they demand honor for themselves. They wear their prayer shawls, not to turn their hearts to God, but to turn other eyes toward them. They demand front seats, not to serve the rest, but to be served. Jesus condemns them to the severest sentence.

On the other hand, the example of a truly faithful person in Judaism is the poor widow. She is willing to contribute what she has to live on, to lay down her life, for the sake of the leaders of the believing community. She does not judge them, perhaps cannot judge them. She simply gives.

Jesus makes two judgments about the situation. He criticizes and condemns some members of the religious establishment who prey on the faith of the devout and lead them to contribute beyond their means. Jewish tradition is consistent in declaring that charitable contributions should be within the means of the giver (see Sirach 35:9-10). The activity of some of the scribes is not consistent with the tradition.

Second, Jesus judges the gift of the woman as the most valuable of all, since she has indeed given her life. Jesus himself will offer his life as a sacrifice for all, without judging whether they deserve the gift. His perfect sacrifice takes away sins once for all (Hebrew 9:24-28).

Irene Nowell, OSB

Questions for Discussion

1. "God doesn't ask us to judge. He asks us to give to support His work," one woman said to the TV reporter after the evangelist she was supporting was convicted of fraud. What do you think of this woman's response? Is her attitude supported by today's readings?

2. Studies show that, proportionately, poor people give more to the Church than do wealthy people. Why do you think this is true?

For Journaling

When I think about giving from my want rather than my surplus, . . .

1. I give of my time to God when I . . .

2. I give of my talent to God when I . . .

3. I give of my treasure to God when I . . .

Christ Dwells among Us

Readings: **Isaiah 56:1, 6-7; 1 Peter 2:4-9; John 4:19-24, or any readings from the Common of the Dedication of a Church**

All of us have places that are special to us. It may be the place where we met our husband or wife. It may be the place where we spent precious hours as a child. It may be a favorite place to think or to pray. Every culture and every religion has sacred places, places where God seems closer than in other places.

The Hebrew Scriptures tell us that God has from the beginning sought a way to be among His people. But while the temple was a sacred place where God could be found, God could never be contained there. Today we celebrate the dedication of the church of St. John Lateran, the cathedral in Rome where the pope, the bishop of Rome, is pastor. The feast celebrates not just a building, but the universal Church gathered with its pastor.

As we celebrate this feast, we remember all the places where Christians gather to worship. We remember the tent of meeting in the time of Moses and the temple in Jerusalem. We remember those first meeting places in homes, in catacombs, in the church meeting halls in imperial Rome, in the glory and majesty of the cathedrals of the Middle Ages and of today. We remember our own parish church, built by our forefathers and foremothers in faith, scene of so many important events in our lives. These are places where we have met our God.

The church of St. John Lateran was originally a public meeting hall for the Roman people. On November 9, 324, the building was dedicated as a church for the Christians. This was the first public church building Christians were allowed to have. Before that time, it was against the law in Rome to be a Christian. People were often put to death for being Christians. They met in secret places to worship, often in tunnels under the city of Rome called catacombs. When the church of St. John Lateran was rededicated in honor of St. John the Baptist, Christian people were once again able to gather to remember and celebrate the presence of God in their lives in a public way.

But even as we celebrate the dedication of a church building today, we are strongly reminded that the presence of God is not assured by a stone building. The temple of the Lord which cannot be destroyed, the place where God dwells, is in the hearts of the faithful; "Are you not aware that you are the temple of God and that the Spirit of God dwells in you?" (1 Corinthians 3:16)

There are a number of readings suggested for today's liturgy. The choice is left to those planning the liturgy for each congregation. In each of the suggested readings from the Hebrew Scriptures, we recall the places where the Hebrew people recognized and proclaimed the presence of God in their midst. We may read about the stones of the shrine where Jacob dreamed of God's presence (Genesis 28:11-18) or the temple of Solomon where the ark of the covenant resided (1 Kings 8:20-23, 27-30; 2 Chronicles 5:6-10, 13-6:2; Ezekiel 43:1-2, 4-7). Isaiah the prophet proclaims, "For my house shall be called a house of prayer for all peoples" (Isaiah 56:6-7).

In the second reading there is a strong reminder that God's presence is not contained in or confined by a structure of bricks or wood or stone. In each of the suggested readings, Paul strongly reminds the Gentile people and each one of us that God resides within. We are the temple, the building, the living stones. The true place wherein God abides is the body of Christ, the community of believers, including each one of us.

Physical structures such as churches, basilicas, and shrines can be replaced or destroyed, but in the shrine of our hearts and in the community of believers, God's presence abides. A visit to a church or cathedral or shrine can remind us of how God has been present and journeying with us throughout history. These places of worship are symbols of God's abiding presence in our own lives and in the life of the Church, the community of believers.

When humans build and dedicate a place of worship, a church, a temple, or shrine to God, we also dedicate ourselves: to God and to one another. The gospel readings remind us of how we are to come into the presence of God and one another in worship.

The building we commemorate in today's liturgy is the church where the pope is pastor. It is a reminder of our connection with the Church and the bishops throughout the world. This basilica, which has been partially destroyed and rebuilt many times, can serve to remind us of the indestructible presence of God.

Jeanita F. Strathman Lapa

Questions for Discussion

1. What is the most beautiful church you have ever visited? Why did you think it was beautiful? How did you feel?

2. How can a church building serve as a symbol of our relationship with God? What does our parish church say about our community of faith?

3. A church building is the place where the Church gathers. How do we recognize the presence of God in the people when we celebrate the Eucharist?

For Journaling

1. The place where I feel closest to God is . . .

2. When I sit in our parish church . . .

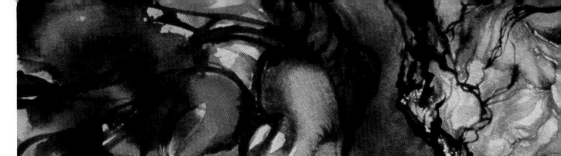

The Lord Will Come

Readings: Daniel 12:1-3; Hebrews 10:11-14, 18; Mark 13:24-32

Every so often someone proclaims that the end of the world is going to come next week or next month at a certain time or a certain day. We have grown used to the prediction and used to the scenery and activity that we think will accompany the end of the world. Where did our ideas of the scenery and activity come from? What is the foundation of such predictions?

Our images of the end of the world come from a worldview called *apocalyptic*. This worldview became strong in Judaism in the persecution of the second century B.C.E. and has flourished since then in other times of persecution. Because of the intensity of the persecution under Antiochus IV (which also inspired the Maccabean Revolt, 165-142 B.C.E.), the idea grew that human history was too corrupt to ever be redeemed. History would have to come to an end. God's salvation would begin within history but would reach completion only beyond history. The power of evil was greater than human strength. Only a great cosmic battle between God and Satan, good and evil, angels and demons, could bring relief from suffering and vindication to the righteous. Since creation also suffered from evil, a great destruction of nature would occur, and new heavens and a new earth would be born out of the conflict. Since human beings could not survive such a cosmic upheaval, the righteous who were to be vindicated would rise again after death.

The Book of Daniel was written during the persecution under Antiochus IV. After the prediction of the great destruction of all human kingdoms (corrupt by definition), Daniel 12 portrays the victory. Michael, the angel, will defend the righteous. Those who deserve vindication will rise from death to life everlasting. This is the first and clearest statement concerning resurrection from the dead found in the whole Hebrew Scriptures or Old Testament. It is the first time the phrase *everlasting life* is used.

Early Christian tradition capitalized on apocalyptic imagery. Jesus, firstborn from the dead, was a witness to the truth of resurrection and the pledge of hope for all believers. The destruction and persecution surrounding the fall of Jerusalem to the Romans in A.D. 70 seemed to many to be the final cosmic battle between good and evil. Jesus' words concerning the coming of the Son of Man in glory to consummate the kingdom of God seemed on the point of fulfillment.

The author of the Gospel of Mark expresses the urgency and need for vigilance felt at this time when Christ might return at any moment. Chapter 13 is an apocalyptic discourse linking the events of the destruction of Jerusalem with the expected second coming. The imagery of cosmic catastrophe surrounds the expectation. Jesus will return as the Son of Man, a figure introduced by Daniel (7:13), who would come on the clouds to receive the kingdom. This figure was developed by later apocalyptic literature (1 Enoch) as the judge of the righteous and the wicked.

Jesus' once-for-all victory over sin and death (Hebrews 10:18) is that in which we already share and that for which we await the final and full realization (Hebrews 10:13). The believer must be ready. Just as the signs of spring tell us to be ready for summer, so the signs of impending disaster warn of the judgment to follow. What day, what hour it will come, no one knows. It is not necessary to know; it is not necessary to predict. It is necessary only to be ready.

Irene Nowell, OSB

Questions for Discussion

1. The cycle of life and death that we witness in nature each season turns our thoughts to our own cycle of living and dying. How does nature give us insight into the hope and promise of God's gift of eternal life?

2. What is your vision of the endtimes? On what is your vision based? What feelings does this raise in you? What is most important to remember about the endtimes?

3. Have you ever met anyone who takes the apocalyptic writings literally? How does this approach obscure the meaning of the Scripture?

For Journaling

1. Whenever I think about my own dying, I feel . . .

2. Heaven is . . .

3. When Jesus comes . . .

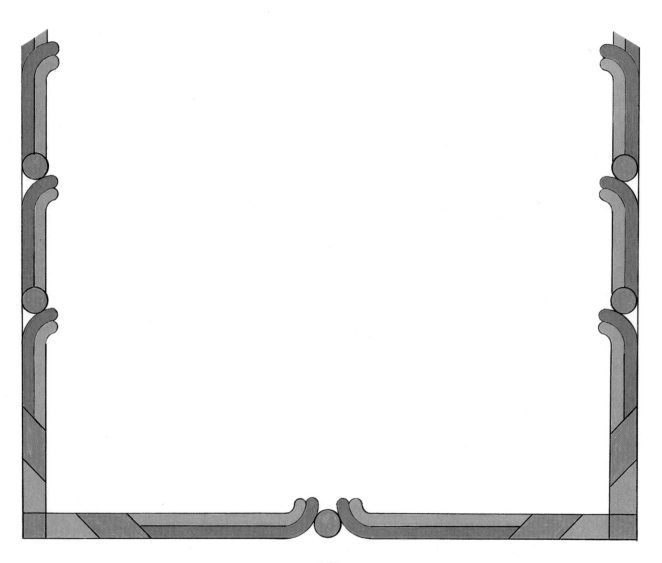

Christ the King

Jesus Christ Reigns

Readings: **Daniel 7:13-14; Revelation 1:5-8; John 18:33-37**

Two of the three readings for this Sunday are taken from apocalyptic writings: the Book of Daniel and the Book of Revelation. The third is from the Passion narrative of Jesus, in which he is in conflict with both religious and political authority. Thus the readings for Christ the King confront us on the one hand with a worldview that God's redemption will come from beyond human history and on the other hand with an image of conflict between Christ and established authority. Christ as King can certainly not be seen in continuity with any historical power.

The reading from Daniel is part of a vision concerning the victory of God's kingdom over all human kingdoms. The human kingdoms are envisioned as four violent beasts coming from the sea, the domain of primeval chaos. The kingdom of God appears as a human being ("son of man" = one in human form) who comes from heaven, God's domain. A judgment scene occurs. God, portrayed as a dazzling fiery Ancient One (cf. Ezekiel 1-3), takes the throne and condemns the beasts to loss of power and to ultimate destruction. Then everlasting kingdom, power, and glory are presented to the human being ("son of man"). In the interpretation of the vision (Daniel 7:15-27), the human being is identified as "the holy people of the Most High" (7:27).

Some parts of later Jewish tradition understood the "son of man" as an individual who would come to restore the kingdom to God's people at the time of the great cosmic destruction. The Son of Man would judge all people and separate them into those who were worthy of God's everlasting kingdom and those who were not. This figure of the Son of Man became a way for Christians to explain who Jesus was, the human being who came from heaven and brought the kingdom of God. On his return he will appear as the Son of Man, coming on the clouds, to bring the fullness of God's kingdom.

The Book of Revelation, written during the Roman persecution at the end of the first century A.D., looks forward to the return of Jesus and the establishment of God's kingdom. Jesus is portrayed as the Son of Man, the witness to the truth of resurrection, and the hope for everlasting life. He has already passed through the great destruction of death and freed us from the power of death, which is sin. He is the victor over all earthly kings and has made God's people into a royal nation. God's royal nation is a nation of priests, those called to minister and to offer sacrifice for all people. When Jesus returns to bring the kingdom in its fullness, then God, the ultimate holder of power, will reign. It is God who is the beginning and the end, who rules for all time.

The Gospel of John presents quite a different picture. During his lifetime, Jesus bears the title of king only at his most vulnerable moments, in his infancy (Matthew 2:2; cf. Luke 1:32) and at his crucifixion (Matthew 27:11, 29, 37; Mark 15:2, 12, 18, 26; Luke 23:2-3, 38; John 18:33-37; 19:3, 14-15, 19-22). In the Gospel of John there is a long discussion between Pilate and Jesus concerning the meaning of the term, *king of the Jews*. Jesus removes the title from the political world of Pilate: "My kingdom is not of this world" (John 18:36). Christ reigns in a different realm than Pilate. Christ is king in the ongoing battle against sin, evil, and death.

Irene Nowell, OSB

Questions for Discussion

1. Can you name places in the world where Christians are not free to practice their faith? What choices must these Christians make?

2. Do you think Christ is King in our country? What would that mean?

3. Have the demands of your faith ever come into conflict with the laws of your country? What would you do if this were to happen?

For Journaling

1. To put Christ before all else means . . .

2. When I think about Christ as King, . . .

3. I help further the kingdom when I . . .